DATE DUE

Str

Fo

NATIO   3

Editor:

DEMCO 38-297

Published by: National Business Education Association
1914 Association Drive
Reston, Virginia 22091

STRATEGIC PLANNING FOR THE 1990's

Copyright 1990 by

NATIONAL BUSINESS EDUCATION ASSOCIATION
1914 ASSOCIATION DRIVE
RESTON, VIRGINIA

$12.00

LIBRARY OF CONGRESS CARD NO. 90-061616
ISBN 0-933964-31-5

Preface

Education for and about business has traversed an adventurous path over the past several decades. The vast revisions in curriculum and diversity of programming have been driven, in part, by change and technology. Information resources and accessibility have broadened the spectrum of learning and working in our society. The free enterprise system has dictated a broad cadre of knowledge and skills that can transfer from one career to another. Leadership, critical thinking, decision making, communications, human relations, and entrepreneurial skills have become vital to job success.

Business educators have the best resources and opportunities to provide meaningful learning experiences within this environment. This 1990 NBEA Yearbook is focused on providing a realistic framework for business educators to face the issues of a new decade and beyond.

The 16 chapters have been organized into three major sections. Part I, "Business Education in Challenging Times," sets the stage for accomplishing change by providing a perspective of the history and growth of business education. Both external and internal influences are addressed from local, regional, and national, and international viewpoints.

The authors contributing to Part II, "Accomplishing Change in Business Education," have taken a practical approach to the issues by discussing program content, teaching strategies, curriculum models, and exemplary programs that really work. A realistic view toward reaching high-risk populations and internationalizing business education provides readers with a good base for program planning, development, and implementation.

In Part III, "Foundations of a Solid Future for Business Education," readers are given ways to actively pursue research, to become politically and legislatively astute, and to establish mutually beneficial partnerships. Suggestions are presented to further personal and professional growth and development—to become goal-oriented professionals and to take advantage of the many windows of opportunity.

All 34 authors contributing to *Strategic Planning for the 1990's* are to be commended for sharing insightful, timely, and practical information. Readers will find a common theme throughout the book—namely that business educators have staked a significant claim in educating our future work force.

Sharon Lund O'Neil, Editor

Contents

PART III
FOUNDATIONS OF A SOLID FUTURE FOR BUSINESS EDUCATION

Part I

CHAPTER 1

A Business Education Perspective: Past . . . Present . . . Future

J. CURTIS HALL

Virginia Commonwealth University, Richmond

Nothing in life is more certain than change. All living things grow, mature, and die. Some exist for hours, some for days, some for weeks, some for months, and some for many years. All, however, are changing constantly, even though the changes may not be readily apparent. Change is never ending, too, in the inanimate physical world. Rivers carry away soils, mountains of stone erode, air currents create changing weather, building materials corrode and decay, and the air is no longer pure. The only unknowns are the direction and the rate of the changes.

Change is ever present in education, also. Goals and expectations of education professionals differ from one period of time to another. So do the aspirations and objectives of students and their parents. Needs and desires of employers do not remain constant, either. Business education is especially subject to changes taking place in society because of its unique mission. Therefore, it may be useful to take a look at where business education has been, where it is now, and where it may be tomorrow.

THE SEARCH FOR IDENTITY

What kind of education, for what purpose, and for whom? These are age-old questions faced by all educators since the creation of the first organized school. The questions never change over time, but the answers do. There is a never ending search by each segment of the education establishment to find its own place in the sun. Typically, the greatest prestige seems to go to those subject fields that were offered first in the schools. They acquire a position of preeminence from which it is very difficult to dislodge them. New fields of study or new courses must fight for a place in the established order. They must justify their right to exist in ways that the early arrivals were not required to do. So it has been with the study of education for business whether at the high school, the postsecondary school, or the collegiate level. Only in very recent years has business education begun to be accepted as an equal among the established academic disciplines in the colleges and universities. In the high school, business education still does not enjoy equal standing with the college preparatory subjects. The search has been for an identity that has significance and lasting value.

1

The purpose of business education programs. The initial thrust of business education in the high school was to help young people learn to do better some of the things they would have to do anyway. Of course, there was the hope that some of them would be able to reach beyond what they might have been able to do without the education. The early focus was on preparing students for work in the business office, primarily at the clerical level. It was not confined to the development of occupational skills, however, and also included the development of general "business knowledge." At first such general knowledge was seen as necessary for proper performance on the job. Later, when jobs were less plentiful, the general business knowledge was promoted for its positive benefit to consumers. It was supposed to help future adults become more rational consumers of economic goods. This general knowledge of business also was supposed to create better citizens by helping people make wiser choices about economic matters when they enter the voting booth.

In the late thirties still another objective of education for business was added to high school programs. It was to prepare students for selling jobs, primarily in the retail industry. Such study became known as distributive education, and its proponents often fought hard to see that it remained separate and distinct from already established business programs. The distinction was due primarily to special funding from the federal government for these "distributive" programs. Years later when federal funding was made available to what had previously been called business education, some insisted that the term "office" education be used to identify programs financed by the new legislation. In the minds of some educators there always needs to be a clear distinction between general education and education for work. Presumably, they believe that which is more general has greater value.

The purpose of business education at the postsecondary level, meaning somewhere between the high school and the four-year college or university, has generally been quite similar to that in the high school. There has been, perhaps, less emphasis on general education at this level and more on job preparation. It has been easy for these institutions, whether they be proprietary schools, technical schools, or community colleges, to assume that their students have already acquired sufficient general education in the high school. The kinds of jobs for which their students are being prepared are essentially the same as those for which the high school purports to prepare its graduates. There is the general expectation, however, that the graduates of these postsecondary schools will be somewhat more mature and that their job skills may be developed to a higher level. Business programs in these schools generally have not had to be quite as defensive about their goals as have those in high schools or colleges and universities. They have had greater freedom in charting their own course, but the results have not been greatly different from those in schools with greater restrictions.

During the early part of this century, education for business at the collegiate level was suffering from its own identity crisis. The struggle, again, was to identify the central purpose of business education. Should it be primarily general education, or should the focus be on preparation for specific careers in business? Students generally gravitate toward programs that offer reasonably specific preparation for work life after college, while the established educators usually opt for the kind of knowledge that is most worthy of being transmitted to the cream of society. The fact that the educators cannot agree among themselves about what knowledge is most worthy never seems to bother many of them. The net result has been that collegiate schools of business have tended to try to serve the dual purposes of general education and professional job preparation. There has always been some disagreement about the proper balance between the two, however.

The content of business education programs. Obviously curriculum content and course content should be directly related to the purpose of an educational program. Usually there is a very close tie between purpose and content when a new program or a new course is initiated. It could hardly be otherwise, because it is the purpose that drives the creation of the new content. Educators who wish to prepare clerk-typists observe what clerk-typists do, then devise course content that will develop the required skills. Those who seek to develop more effective consumers identify the problems that consumers face, then construct courses to help students cope with such problems. Those interested in improving citizenship study what the typical citizen is expected to do, then create content that will accomplish that purpose. The process is sensible and practical. The only major obstacle is to convince the establishment that the new objective and the new content are worthy of being included in the school curriculum.

Once programs and courses are established, however, stated purposes and content tend to drift apart. While the objective of preparing stenographers may remain constant, the skills needed to be effective on the job change. Educators often are reluctant to alter program content to meet the new need. Some courses continue to be taught simply because they have been taught in the past. It is much easier, in some ways, to add new courses than it is to get rid of old ones. For example, the conventional office machines course remained in school programs long after the need for it had passed. The same is probably true of shorthand today.

Sometimes stated objectives for a program or course change over time. The general business course provides a good illustration. The original purpose of the course was to prepare potential high school dropouts for junior office jobs, and content suitable for that purpose was devised. Later the stated purpose of the course was to prepare students to be more efficient consumers. Then the objective shifted to preparation for effective citizenship. Still later the avowed purpose was to develop economic understanding. During much of that time, however, the content of the course remained essentially unchanged. Only in relatively recent years has there been a significant change in the content of the course. Nowhere in business education has the search for identity of purpose and content been a greater struggle than in the so-called basic business area. Even though the need for a better understanding of how the American business system operates is unquestioned, few business teachers seem to want to take on the job of helping to develop it.

These kinds of problems exist, also, at the collegiate level. College faculties like to create new courses, but they are very slow to delete any of the old ones. Course content takes on an importance of its own simply because it has been taught before. Individual faculty members fight for retention of their "specialties" even when the need for them is questionable. The content of undergraduate business degree programs has consisted for many years of two major components. There have been general education, or liberal arts, requirements and professional, or business/management-oriented, requisites. More often than not over the past quarter of a century, undergraduate business programs have been criticized for insufficient breadth of content. Business school accreditation standards have attempted to move curriculum content away from specialization toward greater breadth. At least a part of the reason for that push has been the desire to have the business school gain greater acceptance among the established disciplines in the university.

THE BROAD SPECTRUM OF BUSINESS EDUCATION

It is obvious from the preceding discussion that business education means many things to many people. It is both education about business and education for work in business establishments. It has general education components and specialized vocational or professional education elements. A part of the difficulty in dealing with the topic results from a lack of precision in the definition of terms. Not all of the education that takes place under the label is really related to the private business sector. Much of it has to do with the development of knowledge and skills that can be applied in a wide variety of settings and institutions. Some of it is for the personal benefit of individuals and has nothing to do with employment or career objectives. Most of it, however, relates in some way to "business activities."

Levels of business education offerings. People of all ages are involved now in learning about the business system and in developing skills that are associated with business activities. There are formal programs in schools from kindergarten through the doctoral level in universities. There are informal programs run by churches, professional organizations, and business firms. All have something of value to offer.

Many elementary and middle schools around the country have been involved for years in the economic education movement. Young children are learning about the laws of supply and demand and how they are affected by them. They are learning about the financial services industry through visits to banks or by playing the "stock market game." Some elementary and middle school students are learning keyboarding skills so they can use more effectively the wonderful new machine called the microcomputer.

Junior high schools offer instruction in the use of keyboards that presently provide the major gateway to the use of computers. Some of them also offer courses called introduction to business or general business. Many participate in programs, such as Junior Achievement, designed to develop an appreciation of the private enterprise system. Some also incorporate elements of the economic education program sponsored by the Joint Council on Economic Education and the various State Councils.

4

In recent years high school business programs have made substantial additions to their offerings. The focus is still on preparation for work immediately following graduation from high school, and major attention is given to the development of computer skills. Courses related to understanding the business system appear in most course listings, but enrollments in them are not large.

Business programs in postsecondary schools usually adjust fairly rapidly to changes in job requirements. They add new courses with relative ease in response to what is happening in the external environment. Consequently, their course offerings tend to be extensive and specific.

Enrollments in four-year undergraduate business programs have grown tremendously during the past 20 years. Many business schools have had to limit admission to their programs because of lack of resources to handle the large numbers. Enrollments in graduate business programs have grown even faster on a proportional basis. The MBA degree is a coveted prize and is offered by hundreds of colleges and universities. The number of universities offering the Ph.D. degree in business is also growing. Course offerings have tended to expand as enrollments have increased.

General versus specific education. Both the objectives and the content of business education programs have tended to start with the very specific and move toward the general. At almost every level, early courses usually have been descriptive or "how to" types of offerings. Courses in the high schools and postsecondary schools that are designed to develop specific job skills have generally retained that character. Attempts have been made in some instances to develop a broad view of the job in which the skills will be applied. There is a tendency, also, to structure the course content to develop as wide a range of job skills as possible.

Business degree programs at the collegiate level have moved steadily from the descriptive, specialized nature of early offerings to broad conceptual understandings. Undergraduate degree programs are about evenly balanced between general education and professional education. There still is debate about how much breadth and how much specialization is appropriate, but a majority of faculty and administrators in business schools appear to be satisfied with the current balance.

CURRENT STATUS OF BUSINESS EDUCATION

What is the current state of the art in business education? It is in many ways, quite different from what it was 20 or 30 years ago. In other ways, little has changed. An examination of current program and course offerings may be useful.

High schools. The number of course offerings at the high school level has increased considerably in recent years. The following is a list of the "business" courses described in a 1989 publication of the Department of Education of the Commonwealth of Virginia.

Accounting
Accounting Computer Applications

Applied Business Economics
Applied Business Law
Business Artificial Intelligence
Business Computer Applications
Business Computer Careers
Business Education for the Handicapped
Business Management
Business Supervision and Management
Clerical Accounting I
Clerical Accounting II
Computer Concepts
Data Processing I
Data Processing II
Employment Seminar
Information/Word Processing
Keyboarding
Keyboarding Applications
Legal Office Procedures
Management Information Systems
Medical Office Procedures
Office Assistant
Office Services I
Office Services II
Office Services III
Office Specialist I
Office Specialist II
Office Systems
Recordkeeping
Secretarial Administration I
Secretarial Administration II
Shorthand

As the list demonstrates, there is the possibility of 35 different high school business course offerings in this state. Most of the courses carry one unit of credit, some give two units, and a few are good for only one half unit. Schools are free to choose among them, of course, and no school offers all of them. Some do offer 15 or more of the courses, however. A student who wishes to complete a business program must take a minimum of two and a half units from this list. Some business sequences require a minimum of five units, or nearly one-fourth of the total high school graduation requirements. It is clear that the high schools are offering a large number of very specialized business courses. Roughly one-third of the courses in the list can be identified by title as having computer-related content. An additional one-third mention computer skills in the course descriptions.

Postsecondary schools. Program and course offerings in the postsecondary schools are even more specialized than in the high schools. Following is a list of business or business-related associate degree programs in one community college.

Accounting
Banking and Finance

Business Administration
Business Management
Data Processing
Hotel/Restaurant/Institutional Management
Marketing/Merchandising
Office Systems Technology

The same institution offers the following business-related certificate or diploma programs.

Accounting
Business Credit and Collections
Certified Professional Secretary Preparation
Clerical Office Assistant
Data Entry Operations
General Insurance
Hotel/Motel Management
Insurance Administration
Management Development
Middle Management Development
Office Practices for Educational Personnel
Office Systems Technology
Professional Legal Secretary Preparation
Real Estate
Savings and Loan Administration
Small Business Management
Word Processing

Altogether there are 25 different business-related instructional programs offered by this single community college. Supporting those 25 programs are 284 different courses, each worth three to four quarter-hours of credit. The courses are offered under eight labels, ranging from Accounting to Real Estate. Business Management and Administration offers 63 different courses, and Office Systems Technology wins the prize with 91 separate courses.

All the associate degree programs, except Business Administration, are labeled Associate in Applied Science and require a minimum of only 25 percent of the work in general education. The certificate and diploma programs require only 15 percent of the work to be in general education. The business courses themselves are quite specialized as the following sample of course titles indicates.

Human Relations and Leadership Training
Principles of Credit Union Operations
Deposit Operations
Teller Operations
Bank Cards
Trust Management
Personnel Management
⌐Proofreading and Editing Skills
Medical Typewriting
Agents Life and Health Training
Marketing for Bankers
Fashion Show Production

Colleges and universities. Undergraduate business offerings in the colleges and universities are extensive also. It is not uncommon for a business school to offer eight or ten different degree programs. In addition, there may be "tracks," or subprograms, within each degree. A perusal of one university bulletin revealed an offering of 118 undergraduate business courses and an additional 27 courses in economics. Some of those courses are quite specialized, but much less so than those in the community colleges. Most of the courses are offered in the third and fourth years of the college program when students are presumably more mature and have had a foundation of general education courses. A typical undergraduate business program is about equally balanced between courses in business and economics and courses in general education or liberal arts.

BEYOND TOMORROW

Most Americans have difficulty taking the long view. The usual orientation is toward today and, perhaps, tomorrow. Long-range planning does not come naturally in a world dominated by youth and by quarterly reports to stockholders who are interested in immediate results. Yet, events are taking place now that will shape the future. The trick is to develop a sensitivity to current happenings that will provide a vision for the future. World events of today will have an enormous influence on life beyond tomorrow. Education will have to be responsive to the changes now taking place.

Changes taking place in the world. Everybody talks about today being the new age of technology. And so it is! There are hundreds of new "gadgets" designed to make life easier or more pleasant for individuals. Hundreds more are increasing productivity by either replacing human labor or supplementing it. People must adjust to an environment in which inanimate objects play a leading role. What is more, they must learn to control and use these new devices in their homes and in the workplace. Most of the new technology is directly related to or made possible by the computer. Especially important has been the miniaturization of that powerful tool. People now wear tiny computers on their wrists to tell time and use computers in their automobiles to control engine performance. Paper work and recordkeeping in the office are controlled almost entirely by computers.

The television sets people watch, the radios they listen to, many of the cars they drive, and hundreds of other products they use are no longer made in America. They come from other countries all around the world. Even those that are made in this country may be manufactured by a foreign-owned company. The economy has become a truly global one, and Americans are no longer in charge. Some economists now use the concept of gross world product (GWP) instead of the familiar gross national product (GNP). The United States no longer holds industrial supremacy in the world. It seems likely that third world countries, which have abundant and lower-paid work forces, will dominate industry in the future. Worldwide competition is a fact of life that American business firms, labor unions, and consumers alike must recognize. American companies must also seek markets in foreign countries, which means that Americans must learn about and become more sensitive to other cultures around the world.

The composition of the work force is changing. The trend is toward aging as the bulge of the baby boom population (the 70 million people born between 1946 and 1964) grows older. These workers will begin to approach retirement within the next 20 years. Women now make up about 45 percent of the labor force, and the proportion is likely to increase in the future. The steady increase in white-collar and high-technology production employment opportunities will increase the number of women who work. More minorities and more people from different cultures also are filling all kinds of jobs. The resulting cultural differences among workers create new problems for management and require different working relationships. They may force people to think in totally different ways about their jobs.

The American economy has moved into what has been called the post-industrial age. It is a phenomenon similar to what happened to agriculture in the industrial revolution. Industrial output may not be declining, but the number of people employed in manufacturing jobs is. More people are employed in service jobs than any other kind. The result is a shift from an industrial society to an information society. People are no longer struggling physically against nature or against machines. They are competing mentally against each other. Major changes in where people work, the hours they work, how they are supervised, and how they are paid are in the offing. This new order is coming to be known as the service/information economy.

The nature of the service/information economy is bringing about an increase in the number of small business firms. It has been described as a new wave of entrepreneurism which puts the emphasis on individuality. Since the new industry is brain intensive, rather than capital intensive, it is easier for individuals to strike out on their own. Many of them start out by moon-lighting from regular jobs while they build their own firms to a profitable point. This new spirit of entrepreneurism, plus the computer revolution, undoubtedly will contribute to more people working at home and connecting with employers or clients through telecommunication links.

Implications for business education. What do all these changes suggest for the future of business education? Certainly, there is no shortage of predictions about the future. Some of them seem to be pure fantasy, while others demonstrate a strong tie to history. No prediction about the future is likely to be very accurate, but one based on what is happening now and what has happened in the past probably has a better chance of some success than any other.

Taking into account what is known about the past and the present, some future directions for business education seem apparent. There is an assumption, of course, that business education will continue to perform the dual function of providing both general and job-oriented education. While they may not provide the general education themselves, it is the duty of business educators to design curriculums that ensure a sensible, broad general education for all students. Most of what needs to be done in education for business applies to all levels of study, although the depth and complexity of the work will certainly be different at each level. The business offerings must be practical and related to the workplace outside the school, but they must also be broad enough to enable students to adapt quickly to change. The acquisition of knowledge of specific subject matter probably is not nearly as difficult as the development of essential nonintellectual skills.

What kinds of competencies are needed for the future? They probably are the same ones people have always needed in order to adapt to constantly changing environments. At the very least, business educators of the future must make certain that their students—

- Learn about cultures other than their own.
- Know something about the history, geography, politics, and economy of countries and regions outside the United States and can locate them on a map.
- Are able to communicate reasonably well both orally and in writing.
- Have at least one specific job skill that will enable them to be productive immediately.
- Have experience working with others.
- Learn how to resolve conflicts in work settings.
- Develop an attitude of pride in workmanship.
- Develop critical-thinking and decision-making skills.
- Know how to work independently and to take initiative in their work.
- Know how business in general operates and what the environmental constraints are.
- Know that it is normal to have to learn new things on the job almost all the time.
- Learn the importance of service to the "customer" no matter what the job.
- Understand that additional formal or informal education will be necessary.
- Have basic computer skills to input, output, and disseminate information.

The emphasis throughout this discussion has been on educating the whole individual. Those who plan programs and construct curriculum must take responsibility for that. The suggestions are intended to apply to full-time, regular students who are moving through a particular segment of the educational system for the first time.

There is an equal obligation, however, to part-time students in need of specific help where their previous schooling has been inadequate. Society is beginning to demand greater accountability from educational institutions. Public institutions are expected to become more responsive to market demands. The need on the part of individuals and business firms for continuing education is great. High schools, postsecondary schools, and colleges have an obligation to satisfy that need. In many instances they are expected to play a direct role in the economic development of a city, a county, a region, or the country as a whole. Therefore, business educators at all levels must think in terms of launching students in careers, helping them advance, or helping them enter new careers when old ones disappear.

Business programs of the future should probably have fewer courses, with greater emphasis on more integration among different subjects. If educators themselves are unable to relate one subject field to another, how can they expect students to be able to do it? There needs to be less concern among business educators about their own subject matter "territories" and more concern for what is good for students and the public at large. They, too, need to develop a greater sensitivity to needs and desires of the "customer."

Finally, as was implied in the listing of competencies that all students need, greater emphasis needs to be placed in the future on the noncognitive skills. Recent studies by the American Assembly of Collegiate Schools of Business (AACSB) have suggested that greater attention be given to skills and personal characteristics (SAPC's). They include analytical skills, computer skills, decision-making skills, initiative, leadership/interpersonal skills, oral communication skills, planning/organizing skills, risk-taking skills, and written communication skills. While this list was developed specifically for college or graduate students, many of the skills and characteristics are equally important at all levels. Evidence suggests that they can be developed, although not over very short periods of time. That is all the more reason why attention should be given to them early in life. Many of the students who never go beyond high school or postsecondary school will need them. Educators must help develop them.

CHAPTER 2

Econometric Perspectives at Home and Abroad

BETTY J. BROWN and GEORGE MUNDRAKE
Ball State University, Muncie, Indiana

The United States of the 1990's will be a nation characterized by changes in economic activity, in world standing, and in interactive roles throughout the world. The United States now is sometimes described as a nation in which economic activity consists of predominantly service-related industries. In the past, the primary desciptor of the economy was manufacturing, producing hard goods for both this country and countries around the world. Trading with its economic partners resulted in a trade surplus. American goods were known for their quality and quantity, and as a result, the United States was acknowledged as the "richest nation in the world."

Since the sixties and seventies, those descriptors have changed. The United States no longer operates with a trade surplus. No longer are American goods always described as the best on the market. The price of producing American goods has led to multinational companies establishing plants abroad to produce goods for distribution in the United States. Still, an analysis of this country's status must include a number of factors for comparison. The first part of this chapter will consider the nation's economy as a whole, descriptors that may be applied to it, and measures of its success and efficiency. The second part of the chapter will consider the relative position of the United States in the world, particularly in international trade. The third part will focus on implications for business educators in the 1990's.

THE ECONOMY AT HOME

A service economy. The U.S. economy has shifted from a manufacturing economy to a service-producing economy over the past three decades. The service sector is comprised primarily of communications, transportation, public utilities, finance, insurance and real estate, wholesale and retail trade, government, and pure service industries such as business, personal, and health; some include distributive industries as part of the goods-producing sector. Available data provides insight into a shift to the provision of services and away from the production of tangible goods from raw materials as a major focus for the U.S. economy. The portion of the gross national product produced in services has grown dramatically over the decades of the sixties, seventies, and eighties. However the service sector is defined, the data shows a clear long-term growth in this area that will continue through the nineties.

As a portion of overall employment, the share of service-producing industries has grown over the past three decades. Consumers' personal income has come increasingly from the service sector, with the proportion nearly doubling over the past three decades.

While the service portion of the GNP has increased in the United States, production of goods has remained steady. In constant dollars, both durable and nondurable goods as portions of GNP rose during the eighties. Expenditures for durable goods rose as a percentage of total GNP, an indicator that the concept of a "service economy" does not mean the demise of manufacturing in our economy.

Economic strengths of the United States. What factors have contributed to the economic strength of the United States? What implications do those factors have for business education in the nineties? As a "rich" nation, the United States has experienced an entrepreneurial spirit that encourages the formation of business. Corporations account for the largest percentage of business transactions; however, the number of small businesses has been a major factor in the economy through the years. The number of proprietorships in operation has fluctuated from year to year over the past decades; but, in general, as a percentage of total firms in operation, they have been stable.

Mobility of the labor force is a second factor contributing to economic strength. Workers are free to move to labor markets. If their skills are in demand, workers are motivated to move to existing jobs. The private enterprise system, with a basic principle of supply and demand in operation, rewards them if they have skills and expertise in areas of short supply.

The corporate structure and mobility of capital have enabled American business to react to demand for goods and services. Innovative industries responding to new methods, new products, changes in resource supplies, and consumer demand have prospered. Over the years, massive shifts have occurred in the industrial and occupational distribution of the labor force as a result of growth and change.

The quality of the labor force is an important factor in the economy. In general, the quality of the U.S. labor force is among the highest in the world. Workers attain a higher educational level than most other nations, and they work with resources that facilitate their efforts. However, entry-level skill requirements continue to increase as new technologies are implemented.

Productivity is largely attributable to technological advances which enable workers to make more efficient use of all resources. In turn, technology has brought about capital investment; new ideas that will contribute to increased output require investment in new equipment.

Capital investment in productive resources. The extensive use of capital goods and advanced technology are two characteristics of a modern economy. Tools, machinery, large-scale factories, and facilities for storage, transportation, and marketing lead to production of the goods needed. A measure of the modernness of an economy is the amount of capital investment. In times of recession and cutbacks in capital investments, the nation becomes concerned. American corporations increased their investment in capital goods during the 1980's, except during the period of 1982-84.

The composite index of economic cyclical indicators includes an index of plant and equipment contracts and orders. As that index rose, the index of industrial production and of new orders in manufacturing also rose. Increases in those indexes are a measure of the health of the economic system.

Future economic growth depends on an economy's ability to maintain and produce new capital goods. An area of concern for the nineties is the ability of the United States to reinvest income in capital goods and to maintain ownership of capital goods in this country. Issues of foreign investment in U.S. capital will continue to make economic news for the nineties.

Employment patterns and opportunities. As the United States moves into the nineties, what will the job market be like? The composition of the labor force is closely related to the composition of the economic system's output. As the service sector continues to account for a large share of total output, industries providing services will employ more individuals than the goods-producing sector. Health care, education, repair and maintenance, amusement and recreation, transportation, banking, and insurance are among those service-related areas that will grow.

In 1985 approximately 115.5 million persons were part of the civilian labor force. By 1995 that number is projected to grow to 131.6 million; and by the year 2000, 138.8 million persons will be in the labor force. From 1975 to 1985, the number of workers grew by 21.7 million. From 1985 to 1995, the labor force is projected to grow by 16.1 million, with an additional growth of 7.2 million by the year 2000. However, the rate of growth through the nineties will be slower than in the past two decades. From now to 2000, the labor force will grow at 1.2 percent a year, down from a high of 2.7 percent in the seventies. The composition of the work force will change, with more women participating than in the past. In 1985, 44.2 percent of the civilian work force was female; by 1995, that percent will be 46.5 percent; and by 2000, 47.3 percent. The average age of American employees also will increase during the nineties.

Along with the growth in the labor force, there has been an increase in automation and worker training. With that investment, labor productivity will rise and will be reflected in an increased total output and a rise in the standard of living. In service industries, automation is an answer to a shortage of workers in some areas.

THE ECONOMY ABROAD

International trade. Why do nations trade? Generally, international trade is a means by which nations specialize, increase the productivity of their resources, and have a larger total output. The combination of industries in an economic system determines to some extent their ability to produce goods for trade. Industrially advanced nations are in a position to produce capital-intensive goods, such as automobiles, machinery, agricultural equipment, and chemicals. The United States is not in a position to produce a large share of labor-intensive goods, given the relatively high cost of labor, or of land-intensive commodities, given the relatively small ratio of land to human and capital resources. In a global economy, all nations depend on each other for markets for their goods or labor services.

The United States must be concerned with maintaining its position in world trade. One outgrowth of that concern is that capital investment becomes crucial. To produce the goods that the world market will absorb, capital equipment must be maintained. Some major industries in the United States have declined in past decades as they were unable to compete in the world market with newer, more efficient plants and equipment in other countries.

Comparisons with other countries. Comparing the United States statistically with other countries can be done by gross national product, per capita income, and health figures. Some of the trading partners of the United States are Canada, Mexico, France, and Japan. One measure of the success of an economic system often reported to consumers is the per capita income. In a recent year, the United States had one of the highest per capita income figures among the nations of the world. The low income of many less-developed nations is a major concern for the rest of the world. Many problems contribute to poverty in those nations, and solving those problems should be a priority of the world as a whole.

Of the ten countries listed in Table 1, four trading partners of the United States had relatively higher per capita income figures. In contrast, some countries of the world had figures as low as a few hundred dollars or less.

TABLE 1. Gross National Product and Per Capita Income of Selected Countries

Country	Gross National Product (In Millions)	Per Capita Income
Switzerland	97,100.0	$14,408
United States	$4,200,000.0	13,451
France	724.0	13,046
Canada	367,000.0	13,000
Sweden	100,000.0	11,289
Japan	1,900,000.0	10,266
United Kingdom	453,000.0	7,216
USSR	2,000.000.0	3,000
Mexico	126,000.0	2,082
Brazil	250,000.0	1,523

Source: The World Almanac and Book of Facts, 1989.

Among those countries listed in Table 1, in a recent year Brazil sold 25 percent of its exports to the United States, Canada sold 78 percent, Japan sold 37 percent, Mexico sold 60 percent, and the United Kingdom sold 13 percent of its exports to the United States. In turn, the United States exported 22 percent of its goods to Canada, 10 percent to Japan, 6 percent to Mexico, and 5 percent to the United Kingdom. These figures demonstrate the interdependence of nations.

Health statistics are another indicator of the success of an economic system. Nations are concerned about the rate of births, the rate of deaths, and rates of infant mortality. Those factors all contribute to population growth. If a country is unable economically to support its population, large numbers of people suffer from malnutrition or even starvation. Table 2 shows figures on life expectancy, births per 1,000, deaths per 1,000, the percent of natural increase in population resulting from those figures, and the infant mortality rate, measured in deaths per 1,000 live births.

TABLE 2. Birth and Death Rates for Selected Countries

Country	Life Expectancy at Birth		Births Per 1,000	Deaths Per 1,000	Natural Increase (Percent)	Infant Mortality (Per 1,000 Live Births)
	Male	Female				
United States	71.5	78.5	15.5	8.9	.6	10.4
Brazil	60.9	66.0	30.6	8.4	2.2	70.0
Canada	69.0	76.0	14.8	7.3	.7	8.0
France	70.9	79.0	14.1	9.9	.4	8.2
Japan	75.1	80.8	11.4	6.2	.05	6.0
Mexico	63.9	68.2	27.3	5.0	2.2	42.0
Sweden	73.1	79.1	12.2	11.2	.1	3.3
Switzerland	70.3	76.2	11.7	9.2	.2	9.0
USSR	64.0	73.0	19.6	9.7	.9	31.0
United Kingdom	70.2	76.2	13.3	12.2	.01	10.0

Source: The World Almanac and Book of Facts, 1989.

In less-developed countries, the combination of more births per 1,000 in population, high infant mortality rates, and large increases in population resulting from high birth rates has served to make it more difficult to combat the economic ills that beset them. Without resources to meet their own needs, they have no means of entering into world trade and improving their economic status. They are caught in a trap, with no means of improving their situations.

Even in more-developed countries, such statistics as infant mortality rate are a cause for concern. The United States, with its economic resources devoted to health care, still has a higher infant mortality rate than a number of other nations.

U.S. money in world trade. One result of increasing interdependence among nations has been more attention to currencies. In the 1970's the system by which the U.S. dollar was pegged to other currencies was abandoned, and the dollar has fluctuated in value from time to time. When the dollar is "weak," American goods are more readily affordable to other countries; American goods are attractive on the world market, although they bring fewer dollars to American businesses. When the dollar is "strong," on the other hand, its value in terms of other currencies is higher, and American goods become more expensive to foreign markets. Travel abroad for Americans is less expensive, because their dollars translate into more value in foreign currencies. One important measure, then, of world trade is the value of the dollar in other currencies. American exporters and importers are affected by that value. The amount of American goods that other nations can afford to buy is affected; a strong dollar makes American goods more expensive.

Relationships with trading partners. The United States is dependent on other nations for trade. Some products necessary for manufacturing processes are unavailable anywhere in the country. America produces more goods than can be consumed by Americans, particularly in agriculture and capital-intensive industries. A satisfactory trading relationship with a number of countries is a necessity.

What is the expectation for the future in world trade? A serious trade deficit throughout the eighties focused attention on the need to fit into a global economy. The aging of American resources, such as steel mills, focused attention on competitiveness. The United States in the early fifties was the only major nation with an intact industrial base. Since that time, the rest of the world has recovered, and such nations as Japan have built a newer, efficient industrial base.

The trade deficit and a federal budget deficit loom as serious problems that must be addressed for years to come. Much of the borrowed money has gone to pay for imports throughout the eighties. During the decade of the eighties, the United States moved from a surplus in world trade to a serious shortfall. In the fifties international trade accounted for less than 10 percent of America's total production of goods and services. By the late eighties, international trade accounted for 15.7 percent of total goods and services. Imports were about 60 percent of the total, indicative of the trade deficit problem. When imports exceeded exports by such large numbers, larger and larger deficits were accumulated. There is no easy solution to the problem. Because of their interdependence, nations cannot capriciously cut imports to decrease their payments and increase exports to increase their sales. The size and complexity of the world market causes the problem to be of staggering proportions.

Future trade relationships will be crucial to the American economy, perhaps to a greater degree than in the past. Canada, the European Community, Japan, the OPEC nations, Mexico, and other trading partners will absorb goods and services produced by America that cannot be consumed in the domestic market. In turn, those countries provide a source of goods and services that cannot be produced in the United States or that must be traded for the American goods they buy. The future can only bring an increasingly close relationship among all economic systems.

The U.S. share of the world market has shrunk, but total production has not. The number of jobs in America has grown; many industries are expanding; and exports have increased steadily. Economic problems in other countries affect the United States. The problems of Latin American countries, with their heavy debt to the United States, contribute to the trade deficit.

Sources of friction. The global economy must address the problems that arise in connection with the interdependence of nations and increased trade.

Countries find themselves in a "technological race" in a competitive world market. They find themselves caught in the dilemma of serving their own interests at the expense of others, weighing the cost of decisions in the world market. Problems in trade, the world money market, and the environment cause friction.

Trade problems arising from the sale of U.S. products to other countries have raised a cry for protectionism. Attempts at protective tariffs have brought repercussions; a country forced to pay tariffs can also impose tariffs. Sanctions and tariffs can be used as political weapons to voice concerns about other countries' actions. Because the United States imports so many goods, protective tariffs imposed on imports can cause repercussions in exports. Other countries feel compelled to raise their tariffs in response. Such actions contribute to tension and often contribute nothing to a solution; the underlying problem is still the trade gap, a persistent and long-term problem.

A scarcity of resources necessitates trade with other nations. Frictions arise from a shortage of a badly needed resource. The United States, for example, has been heavily dependent on OPEC nations for oil. In the last decade approximately 50 percent of the oil imported by the United States came from OPEC. Even though that percentage was a substantial decrease from the 70 percent or more dependence of the 1970's, it still can be a source of worry and friction.

Environmental problems cause friction. Declines in the peaceful use of atomic energy in the 1980's because of nuclear accidents and the greenhouse effect caused by burning of fossil fuels present nations with important environmental decisions. In addition, acid rain, solid waste disposal, and air and water pollution of all types cause nations to question the good intentions of one another. Such problems remind us that the actions of one do have an impact on others; cooperation is the only way to attack some of the problems that affect all.

Choices that must be made within nations include trade-off effects on other nations. One nation's solution may contribute to another's problems, as illustrated by the Chernobyl disaster of 1986. Dealing with these areas of friction is of high priority as the global economy becomes more real. Political decisions involving trade sanctions or embargoes may in effect create long-range economic difficulties for trading partners with counterproductive results.

IMPLICATIONS FOR BUSINESS EDUCATION

Education in a global economy. What effect does a global economy have on education, particularly business education? As the "world becomes smaller" and communication, trade, and association among countries increases, educational exchange will increase. More foreign citizens will participate in the American educational process as they move to the United States to work with foreign-owned companies. As world trade is expanded, American companies will place more families in other countries to work. Their children will participate in other countries' educational systems. The interdependence that has become a part of the trade picture will become a part of the educational picture, too.

Expectations of workers coming to the United States may cause some change in the American educational system. During the eighties a concern with the quality of American schools was raised when foreign-born children, transplanted when their families were involved with companies expanding operations, seemed to perform much better than American-educated children. In some cases, those families voiced some concerns about differences in the educational systems; their children must progress equally well in the United States so that they keep pace with their classmates in their own country. American citizens in other countries have the same concerns about their children's education.

Skills needed for the future. A major concern about education as the United States enters the nineties is the level of employment skills needed for the future. The alarm was sounded when a network newscast announced that only twenty-five percent of the applicants for jobs by the year 2000 will be qualified for the entry-level jobs available. A measure for the future, since the skill of the labor force is a factor in economic progress, is the preparedness of future workers. With technology, growth of the service sector, and increased sophistication in requirements for positions in the workplace, American workers will be compared to workers in other countries. Such comparisons were a factor in the late 1980's, when growth of Japanese companies caused alarm among some Americans. Were the Japanese continually going to outstrip the United States in economic growth? Were their methods better? Did they increase productivity to the extent that Japanese workers were "better" than American workers? Such concerns inevitably lead to an analysis of employment skills needed for the future.

The educational system has identified certain basic skills that will be crucial for the worker of the 1990's: math, communications, computer skills, reasoning skills, and problem-solving skills. "Back to the basics" as a cry for revamping education is not entirely the solution. Entry-level skills for the nineties will be different in some aspects from those of the past. Entry-level employees must be able to apply the basic skills to on-the-job tasks. Knowing when to use basic skills is as important as knowing how to use them. Technology has led to increases in the levels of basic skills needed for jobs. Reasoning and solving problems are skills that must be developed, beyond the basic reading, writing, and computational skills that have been recognized as critical in the past. More skills are "basic" for the nineties. Business educators will search for ways to develop and integrate reasoning and problem-solving skills into the repertoire of students going into the labor force, as well as continue to develop and refine their communication and computational skills. As job titles change through organizational changes for efficiency and technological integration, basic skills alone are not guarantees of employment.

Educational attainment of the population enables a nation to compare itself with others. Such indicators are not true and indisputable measures of the preparedness of students to reach their potential, but they are the best available. As entry- and reentry-level jobs demand more sophisticated skills, the dropout and graduation rates cause concern. As a percent of the total population, the dropout rate declined during the eighties. However, the thousands of students who left school with few skills to sell in the marketplace can only face more and more problems in fitting into a labor market with higher and higher requirements for employment. In comparison to most other nations of the world, the United States has a high level of education, a high percentage of its population enrolled in school, and a high level of educational attainment. Whether those statistics are a true indicator of preparedness for the nineties is a particularly grave question facing educators.

Many of the factors that encourage economic growth and lead to economic strength are closely related to education. The skill of the labor force, its ability to cope with technology, and the entrepreneurial spirit are influenced by the educational system which prepares workers for the workplace. In the nineties, business education will be faced with a continuing need to adapt to technological change and to prepare its traditional students to adapt to a constantly changing workplace, requiring more skill. Business educators at all levels will also need to provide nontraditional students with training and upgrading to maintain and increase skills for current and future positions.

The computer has been perhaps the biggest change agent for business education over the decade of the eighties. Before then, only a small percentage of business education programs were influenced by technological change. With the advent of the personal computer, electronic typewriters, and word processors, business education at all levels adapted to technology in the office workplace, particularly. Technological progress has been an influence in all areas of the workplace, not just the office.

Technologically, the United States is among the most sophisticated nations in the world. The educational system is subjected to pressures to prepare students with the technological skills they need later in life. During the eighties those pressures led to increased use of computers at all levels of education. Statistics on the number of microcomputers in use at all levels, the extent to which computers were used in instructional programs, and the level of use per pupil were gathered and reported. The number of schools with computers for student instruction rose dramatically, and the ratio of computers to number of students fell, demonstrating that schools were responding to the demand for change.

Responding to a rapidly changing employment world often means more education and training. Through the nineties, if the past indicates a trend, adult education and training programs will continue to be important. The percentage of higher education students who were part-time students increased over the eighties; U.S. government projections for 1995 estimate that 46.8 percent of higher education enrollment will be part time, up from 42.2 percent in 1985.

By 1985, the numbers of higher education students who were "nontraditional," or who were not typical 18- to 22-year-old college students, had risen to 57.42 percent, compared to 53.92 percent in 1980. By 1995, projections are that 62.72 percent of higher education students will be over 22 years of age. Also, by 1995, the percentage of students who are 25 years of age or older will rise. Table 3 shows 1985 figures and projections for 1995.

An older educational population is an indicator of a need for updating, upgrading, and retraining in the marketplace. The need for new skills or upgraded skills to fit the marketplace of the 1990's offers opportunities for business education. Secondary and postsecondary business education programs can offer the needed training.

TABLE 3. Higher Education Enrollment by Age
(1985 and Projected 1995)

Age	1985 (Percent)	1995 Projected (Percent)
22 years or younger	42.59	37.27
22-24	15.78	14.21
25-29	15.95	15.13
30-34	10.30	12.17
35 years and over	15.39	21.21
25 years and over	41.64	48.51

Source: Statistical Abstract of the United States, 1988.

Implications at home. A major concern of our educational system during the 1990's, particularly of business education, must be preparing students with entry-level skills that will enable them to acquire the increasingly more complex jobs that will be available to them. They also must be inculcated with the expectation of lifelong learning, a readiness to adapt to change, and a willingness to develop abilities needed to fill those jobs that evolve from a changing, more interdependent, and increasingly world or global economy.

What is the role of business education in preparing citizens to be a part of this world economy? Isolationism is not the answer. The United States cannot shut itself off from the rest of the world and its problems. Therefore, business education must expand its goals to include an awareness of what it means to live and work in an international economy. As the workplace becomes more complex, requiring higher levels of skills to operate in an increasingly automated environment, students must be prepared to cope. They must be aware that nations are interdependent, that even those areas of the United States which in the past have had little need or desire for contact with other countries now must seek that contact.

Given the type of economic realities that face them, students should meet five goals in their education for business: technological literacy, economic literacy, consumer literacy, occupational literacy, and civic responsibility. Technological literacy will include the basic skills needed to cope with the complex workstation: communications, problem-solving, decision-making, learning, and computer skills, as well as those "traditional" skills that are still needed. Economic literacy will include an awareness of the interrelationships among countries, and the need to understand their interdependence and the individual citizen's interdependence with people of other countries. Consumer literacy will include a sense of the need for imports and exports and how those consumer goods that are traded on the world market fit into the economic picture. Occupational literacy will include an awareness of the changing workplace and of the need for lifelong learning skills. Because new skills open new opportunities, the curriculum must be attuned to the workplace of the 1990's so that students are prepared with those skills and knowledges that enable them to enter more sophisticated jobs. Civic responsibility will encompass much of what this chapter has discussed: an awareness of the realities of living in a global economy, and recognition that our world does change.

The prediction that only 25 percent of the applicants for jobs in the year 2000 will be qualified for the entry-level jobs available to them must not be allowed to come true, particularly in business education, which contributes to the education of an increasing number of employees in the workplace. Alone, this prediction offers business educators a challenge for the 1990's and beyond. Business educators must be willing and able to change curriculum, methods, and attitudes to meet the challenge.

CHAPTER 3

Educational Standards and Reform: Input . . . Revise . . . Output

MICHAEL G. CURRAN, JR.

New Jersey State Department of Education, Trenton

DOLORES CAPRARO GIOFFRE

Montclair State College, Upper Montclair, New Jersey

The 1983 report of the National Commission on Excellence in Education asserted that America had let its formal education deterioriate to such a dangerous degree that we had become a "nation at risk."[1] The report stressed the need to evaluate the United States to a standard of a lifelong learning society where school must be more demanding, suggesting that there is a need in the United States to form an alliance among teachers, education administrators, parents, and other citizens in order to accomplish this task. The report further stated that school requirements must be strengthened, more vigorous and measurable standards must be instituted by schools and colleges and universities, admission standards of colleges and universities must be raised, and the preparation of teachers must be improved so that teaching becomes a more rewarding and respected profession.

MAJOR CONCERNS FACING TEACHER EDUCATORS

The importance of cultural literacy. E. D. Hirsch, in his book *Cultural Literacy: What Every American Needs To Know,* stresses that to be culturally literate is to possess the basic information needed to thrive in the modern world. Such basic information includes the sphere of vocabulary needed for literacy in the English-speaking nations—that core of background information unique to one's nation. In order to reach cultural literacy in our schools, he continues, teachers and administrators must reach agreement about what the common knowledge should be and, then, equip classrooms so that access to classroom materials that impart the core knowledge to students is ensured.[2]

Teacher education essentials. In his "Case Study in Teacher Education," Kenneth T. Henson found that teacher education majors need more classroom experience and more descriptive and analytical feedback about performance during the clinical experiences. He also found that there is a need to con-

---

[1]*A Nation at Risk: The Imperative for Educational Reform.* A report to the Secretary of Education by the National Commission on Excellence in Education. Washington, D.C.: Government Printing Office, 1983.

[2]Hirsch, E.D., Jr. *Cultural Literacy: What Every American Needs To Know.* New York: Vintage Books, 1988.

ceptualize the relationship between teacher preparation and teaching practice. This can be done, according to Henson, by having students who are studying to be teachers examine the common teaching experiences and discuss the principles of teaching behavior by using them. Further, he states that the preparation of teachers requires developing the skills necessary for the identification of a multitude of acceptable, wise decisions; that teachers must develop the ability to separate the pertinent facts from the less significant and insignificant ones.[3]

The move toward a quality workforce. In July 1988, a joint initiative of the U.S. Departments of Labor, Education, and Commerce published a study entitled "Building a Quality Workforce" that addressed the problem of preparedness for work. One hundred thirty-four business representatives and thirty-four educators were consulted "to assess: (1) current and future entry-level worker needs; (2) current and future workforce capabilities; (3) the gaps or mismatches between the skills business needs versus the skills of the entry-level workers actually available; (4) roles and responsibilities of business and educators in preparing the entry-level workforce; and (5) the challenges involved in building collaborative relationships between business and education."[4]

The thrust for the study is summarized in comments from the representative secretaries of Commerce, Labor, and Education. U.S. Department of Commerce Secretary C. William Verity, said that:

Today we appear to be facing—probably for the first time in our history—a potential breakdown in one of the essential links in this chain. In brief, at a time when more and more jobs require at least basic proficiency in English comprehension and mathematics, our young entrants into the labor force are proving to be disturbingly deficient in these skills . . . now we have discovered we have a problem scarcely imagined a few decades ago—the problem of hiring new entrants into the labor force who are capable of performing the work they are hired for.[5]

Ann McLaughlin, Secretary of Labor, voiced similar concerns:

The school systems of America will play the pivotal role—as they have in the past—in determining whether or not our labor force will have the basic skills to meet the requirements of the jobs which will become available. These requirements are changing. The jobs created in the future will be more complex. They will demand better reading, writing, mathematical and reasoning skills . . . there are indications that a skills gap already exists between the emerging job opportunities and the basic qualifications of young people graduating—or in too many cases dropping out of high school.[6]

Former Secretary of Education William J. Bennett referred to the progress the nation has made:

Five years ago, the publication of *A Nation at Risk* awakened the American people

[3]Henson, Kenneth T. "Case Study in Teacher Education." *Educational Forum* 52:235-41; Spring 1988.

[4]*Building a Quality Workforce: Joint Initiative of the U.S. Department of Labor, U.S. Department of Education, and U.S. Department of Commerce.* Washington, D.C., 1988. pp. 3, 4.

[5]*Ibid.,* p. v.

[6]*Ibid.,* p. iii

to the crisis we then faced in our schools. The response to that report was dramatic, widespread and encouraging. Yet we are still far from closing the gap between the needs of the workplace and the education our schools provide . . . In many cities across the country, we are seeing the development of community partnerships that bring new resources to our schools and new commitment to our students. These partnerships can be a vehicle for improving school performance, for building civic literacy, and for creating a workforce prepared to adapt to changes in the workplace.[7]

The joint study concluded that "in order to close the skills gap, we need to: (1) improve the quality of education for our nation's youth through fundamental education reforms in our nation's schools; (2) mobilize businesses to assist schools in ways that capitalize on their comparative strengths and advantages; and (3) mobilize the community—all sectors—to integrate efforts to ensure a quality education for our young people and a quality workforce for our nation."[8]

The relationship to business education. The issues raised by these leaders is not foreign to business education. For years, leaders in business education have been examining and discussing the best ways to teach, prepare teachers, and provide a curriculum that would benefit all. Such concerns are evident in two recent documents published by the National Business Education Association. The *Business Teacher Education Curriculum Guide*[9] and the *Standards for Business Teacher Education*[10] stress the need for greater professionalism in business teacher education, create an awareness of the problems related to business education, and provide a list of standards which might be used to conduct a comprehensive program of self-evaluation that could lead to the improvement and enhancement of business teacher education programs in the United States. In addition, the *Database of Competencies for Business Curriculum Development, K-14* from the National Business Education Association "outlines a model from which schools may draw instructional standards for use in their own programs of instruction."[11] These documents bring together the types of programs that should be offered in the public schools in order to ensure a thorough and efficient education for those students preparing to enter the business world after graduation and for those students preparing to advance their studies in the field of business.

With concern for the best education at the K-12 level and the best teacher education preparation programs possible for those entering the teaching profession, much reform is taking place in the education environment. Radical changes have been made in the way students progress in the K-12 years. Further changes have been made in the way teachers are prepared at the college/university level. And, reform is taking place in the way business

---

[7]*Ibid.*, p. vii.

[8]*Ibid.*, p. 5.

[9]*Business Teacher Education Curriculum Guide.* Reston, VA: National Business Education Association, 1987.

[10]*Standards for Business Teacher Education.* Reston, VA: National Association for Business Teacher Education, 1988.

[11]*Database of Competencies for Business Curriculum Development, K-14.* Reston, VA: National Business Education Association, 1987. pp. 1-3.

teachers are certified for the subject matter in which they teach. This chapter will discuss the current trends in educational reform in the United States, how these reforms have affected business education, how they will continue to affect business education in the future, and how we might work to continually improve our educational process so that all will benefit.

TEACHER TESTING

Testing for certification. Currently a variety of testing methods are being used to validate the qualifications of business teacher education candidates for certification. These findings were the result of a national study conducted by NABTE (National Association for Business Teacher Education) to ascertain the methods by which business teacher education candidates were certified once they had completed the prescribed program of study for business teacher education. Of the 49 states responding to the survey, 25 were already using a teacher examination to certify business teacher education candidates, and 12 of the states planned to require an examination within two years. Of those states requiring an examination now or within two years, 23 indicated they used the NTE (National Teacher Examination) as their certifying instrument; 7 states indicated they had developed their own examination; the other states required examinations in literacy, general education, history, U.S. government, etc.[12]

With state-developed examinations, the study found no consistency as to who prepares them. Many states handled the preparation through an agency such as the state department of education while other states contracted the services of a test development agency such as ETS (Educational Testing Service). In either situation, reform was evident—business teacher education candidates are being certified through testing processes and the number of states requiring an examination is increasing each year. It is safe to assume, therefore, that the early 1990's will see examinations as the instrument for teacher education certification.

The question then arises: How will these new certification requirements affect those teachers who are already certified? It appears that teachers who were previously certified through other methods (e.g., completion of a prescribed college program, completion of specific college courses, one year of successful teaching) will be "grandfathered" in the subjects for which they are currently certified, although they may be required to pass the appropriate examination (if one is required) to receive additional certification.

Use of multimedia packages. There are other methods of examination for teacher certification under consideration at this time. One of those is through the use of multimedia packages. Many multimedia packages are now under development that will replace the traditional paper and pencil examinations currently used. The multimedia package examination will be administered at various times throughout a teacher's education and career. Multimedia

---

[12]*National Business Teacher Examination Study.* Reston, VA: National Association for Business Teacher Education, 1988. p. 2.

packages will make extensive use of technology and will include ways of evaluating the actual classroom performance of teachers. Researchers are predicting that the use of multimedia packages will change the way teachers are assessed. In the future, teachers will be assessed and certified on a continuing basis over their career. Assessment will include tests of knowledge and reasoning, systematic documentation of accomplishments of both teachers and students, statements of colleagues and students as well as parents, and analyses of performance at assessment centers and in the workplace. These elements will be combined and integrated so that they will be a clear representation of a teacher's progress and will measure different competencies.

Multimedia packages will not be the only method used to measure performance of teachers. Researchers are also considering the use of computer technology for testing purposes. This would require the teacher to assume an interactive role with the computer in responding to questions and classroom situations. Not to be forgotten are the traditional observations of classroom performance and portfolios with documentation of teaching performance.

Development of assessment prototypes. Prototypes of assessment methods under development at Stanford University could be ready for use within the next few years. Included in these assessment prototypes is a battery of tests to be administered three times during a teacher's education and early career. The first examination in the battery would be administered to students in the sophomore year of college. This examination would evaluate basic skills and would probably be administered using the computer. The second examination would be administered at the end of the teacher education program and would be a traditional examination that would evaluate the knowledge of subject matter and the principles of teaching and learning. Following a substantial teaching practicum, the third examination would be administered and would include a variety of assessment methods to evaluate the performance of the classroom teacher. The computer and interactive videos might be employed to measure the problem-solving, decision-making, and general management techniques of the classroom teacher.

Use of performance exercises. Test items may not be the single teacher performance assessment device in the future; researchers stress that a test score is not an accurate indicator of performance as complex as teaching. The future will see performance exercises as a measurement of teaching performance. A more realistic gauge, however, might be a portfolio including structured documentation of the students' work, videotapes of teachers teaching, descriptions of teaching by other colleagues, and other items of measurement. Whatever the measure is, the National Standards Board will be instrumental in its acceptance.

Role of the National Standards Board. The National Board for Professional Teaching Standards was established in 1987 by the Carnegie Forum on Education and the Economy to certify school teachers as professionals. The Board recognizes that currently there are no models for evaluating the performance of educators as there are in architecture, law, and medicine.

The Board feels, however, that such models are necessary in the teaching profession and projects that prototypes of such examinations will be available for use soon.

TEACHER CERTIFICATION/RECERTIFICATION

Not only is reform evident in the way teachers are tested for certification, but results of the NABTE study show that many states are moving toward the issuance of one certificate to business teachers who complete the prescribed college program and who meet the examination criteria of the particular state. Currently, 20 states offer one certificate in business education. Some states require a separate endorsement for data processing, and several states consider areas such as shorthand and marketing as "add ons."

Types of certificates. Certificates are awarded at temporary, permanent, or renewable levels. Temporary certificates are issued in some states for a period of one to two years and are renewed with successful classroom teaching as evidenced by evaluations. Most states (45 at this time) issue renewable certificates. The terms by which certificates are renewed and the length of time for renewal vary with every state. Business education certificates are renewed from one- to five-year periods. The terms of renewal range from college credits to attendance at professional meetings and seminars, to participation in in-service programs, to completing the master's degree within a specified period of time. However, currently the trend is away from the issuance of a permanent certificate and the move to a renewable certificate.

Alternate route to certification. Recently, some states have implemented alternative routes to certification for individuals who wish to teach. In most instances, graduates with a baccalauerate degree and a major in the subject matter area being pursued for certification may sit for the National Teacher Examination. Upon successfully passing the examination and after a pre-scribed period of successful teaching and learning, certification is granted in the respective subject area.

New Jersey's alternate route to certification. The New Jersey State Board of Education, in September 1984, adopted the regulations which permit the training of beginning teachers through what is called the Provisional Teacher Program. This program permits local districts to hire candidates for teaching certification who have a baccalaureate degree, a 30-credit major in the appropriate field, and a passing score on the National Teacher Examination in the appropriate subject field. The local New Jersey school district must demonstrate the capacity to operate a one-year full-time training and super-vision program for the candidates.

In the New Jersey Handbook for State-Approved District Training and Supervision Programs, program components are outlined as: (1) approxi-mately 200 hours of formal instruction in the knowledge and skills necessary for effective beginning teachers; (2) supervision and support at prescribed intervals by members of the professional support team during a full-time, year-long provisional teaching experience; and (3) formal evaluation at three points during the training year by specified members of the support team.[13]

It is uncertain at this time how many teachers will seek certification through the alternate route. However, after three years of offering the alternate route, New Jersey has employed 285 provisional teachers. Commissioner of Education, Saul Cooperman has commented that "employing superintendents and principals have indicated that they are impressed with the teachers' grasp of their subjects as well as their ability to adapt to the demands of the classroom."[14] One thing is certain, though—revisions in certification are part of the reform in education and the alternate route to certification is one of those revisions being implemented in many states at this time.

NATIONAL REFORM GROUPS

Work of the Holmes Group. The Holmes Group is one entity that has received a great deal of attention for its recommendations for reconstructing the entire education profession, especially teacher education. Members of the Holmes Group, established in 1985, have been meeting throughout the five identified regions in the United States in an attempt to develop projects aimed at creating substantive changes in the preparation of teachers. Approximately 100 major universities are currently members of the Holmes Group from across the United States. They represent, for the most part, colleges/universities with strong undergraduate teacher education programs and a good foundation for research.

The Holmes Group is seeking a major commitment for the creation of schools in which university people and experienced teachers together can pursue research and development and new ways of teacher preparation. They are advocating the creation of professional development schools with the establishment of professional development centers. Professional development centers would consist of teams of teachers including two classroom teachers, a professor from the participating university, a first- and second-year teacher aide, an intern, and two residents. Working with the prospective teacher, the team would provide an opportunity for a teacher to gain liberal, professional, and practical preparation that is integrated and supervised over several years.

The Holmes Group supports the idea that teacher education is the responsibility of the whole university, not just the schools of education. While it began as an effort to renovate teacher education programs, the Group believes it is necessary to rethink certification of teachers and standards imposed on teacher education programs. They are advocating that the undergraduate degree in education be replaced with a major in the arts and sciences and colleges and universities begin to look at the master's degree as the initial degree for teacher certification. However, instead of just adding the fifth year to the teacher education program, the Holmes Group suggests that the college/university will have to look at the experiences the program offers,

[13]*New Jersey Provisional Teacher Program: Handbook for State Approved District Training and Supervision Programs.* Trenton: New Jersey Department of Education, 1988. p. 1.

[14]*Ibid.*, Introduction.

the blend of academic and clinical experiences, its liberal arts education, and the models of teaching and learning offered for a lifetime of professional development.

The focus of the work of the Holmes Curriculum Committee is development of a framework to encourage thoughtful reflection about the kind of education teachers need. Within this broad outline will be the principles that should be the foundation of any respectable program for prospective teachers. The recommendations being gathered from member institutions include liberal studies and the elements of a good clinical introduction. The Curriculum Committee will focus on what is liberal in the disciplines in its first major report scheduled for release in 1990.[15]

In the meantime, many colleges/universities are already using the findings of the Holmes Group to reform their teacher education programs. They are requiring a fifth year of study as well as clinical experiences in their programs. The 1990's will likely see a move toward an undergraduate major in the arts and sciences with concentration for teacher certification to come after the undergraduate degree. Such a move could easily steer certification of business educators toward one certificate rather than many different certificates as some states are now awarding.

PUBLIC SCHOOL REFORM

Assessment of secondary school students. Educational reform is not only taking place in teacher education programs but has also become an integral part of the public school education process. Many states have developed assessment tests in reading, writing, and computational skills. These tests, administered to all secondary school students, demand a clear and explicit demonstration of proficiency in reading, writing, and computational skills as a minimum for high school graduation. In addition, the assessment requires the development of guidelines for graduation standards by local boards of education as well as remediation procedures for students who fail to meet the graduation standards.

Impact on business programs. Although the implementation of more stringent graduation requirements has produced a body of students with greater levels of proficiency in reading, writing and computational skills, the fallout in business education has increased considerably. While some states allow business courses to count toward graduation credit, others do not. For example, some states permit business mathematics or accounting to count as mathematics credit toward graduation and business English or business communications to count toward the English requirement. Where states do not permit counting these courses, business education courses are experiencing significant decreases in enrollment as students do not have time in their academic programs for elective business courses.

---

[15]Lanier, Judith E., and Featherstone, Joseph. "A New Commitment to Teacher Education." *Educational Leadership* 46:19; November 1988.

Recognition of Carnegie units. Problems also exist in terms of what high school courses can be assigned Carnegie units, those units necessary for admission to college. In some states, while local districts permit business education courses to count for graduation, postsecondary colleges/universities may balk at accepting high school courses if they have not been taught by certificated mathematics and English teachers.

IMPACT ON BUSINESS EDUCATORS

It is clear that business educators must practice efficiency in the classroom and offer a product that is concise and can be marketed. Business educators must recognize that change is evident and that it can be successfully implemented without substantial loss to business education programs. In schools where teachers actively promote business education and offer alternatives to traditional instruction, business education enrollments are being maintained and, in some cases, even increasing. In schools where tradition is the norm and teachers are not working to promote business education, enrollments are, for the most part, on the decline. Business educators must continually address the issue of appropriate certification for the teaching of keyboarding in grades K-8 and must strive to prepare for new and different levels of teaching while serving new and different student populations. These are critical issues in this age of reform if business education is to survive.

ARTICULATION

Additionally important to the survival and importance of business education is articulation at every level. Teachers, parents, administrators, and students must work to develop successful articulation programs. Articulation is critical at every rung of the academic ladder, from elementary to middle/junior high school, to high school, and on to two- and four-year college programs. It is especially important for the lines of communication and collaborative arrangements to be fostered between the two- and four-year college programs. By developing successful articulation programs, business educators will be assured of providing the best program for students at every level, ensuring that study in business education will be carefully planned and properly executed.

CONCLUSION

Educational reform has only just begun! Reports and studies have validated the importance of educational reform at every level and discipline of education, and changes are taking place at a rapid pace. We can sit back and do nothing; or we can work to ensure that our input becomes part of the revision that will become part of the output. As business educators we must recognize, respond to, and be leaders in the educational movements within the nation. As we adapt our programs of instruction to meet the needs of our students, the requirements of our colleges/universities, and the demands of society, we can shape our future. The challenge is ours!

Part II
ACCOMPLISHING CHANGE IN BUSINESS EDUCATION

CHAPTER 4

Knowledge Systems Workers in the 1990's and Beyond

MARIANNE J. D'ONOFRIO

Central Connecticut State University, New Britain

The year is 2010. The knowledge age is upon us. The United States has regained its leadership position in the economic community. It is once again a fierce competitor in the global business environment. This resurgence in economic dominance is the product of synergism resulting from the interaction of many factors that are keys to global competition. These factors include a decline in trade barriers, an increase in international companies producing across international boundaries, an increase in alliances and consortia among international companies, a decline in labor rates, a substantial increase in the number of small, aggressive high-technology companies, the rapid development and exchange of technology, an improvement in the ability of individuals to learn quickly, and the rapid communication afforded by advances in telecommunications and, thus, fewer secrets.

The recognition of the need for this set of factors became evident as the nation approached the year 1990. The nation's economic position was in jeopardy; strategic planning and action were imperative. The nation's economic position precipitated a series of paradigm shifts in the economy, society, and education. By 1990 the economic model, dominated for several decades by the need to preserve a free nation, had shifted to a model dominated by the need to address economic competition. The development of the European common market contributed to this new set of economic dynamics; it provided the impetus for the nation's actions. The term competitive advantage became the nation's byword. Productivity was recognized as the key to competitive advantage.

The desire to improve the nation's competitive advantage compelled the nation to assess the dynamic nature of the society. The move from an information society to a knowledge society brought the emergence of a group of workers called knowledge workers, characterized as adding value to knowledge. This group of workers became the fastest growing segment of the work force in the 1990's. By the year 2000, 21 million new jobs were created in the nation; more than one-half of these new positions required education beyond high school, and more than one-third of the positions required a college degree.

The demographics of the nation's society also shifted. The population began to age; by the year 1990 the median age was 35. Dual-income families were the rule rather than the exception. By the year 2000, 65 percent of all women between the ages of 16 and 68 were employed outside of their households. Ethnic diversity also began to increase; by the year 2000, the ethnic population had become the majority in several states. The nation's population began moving away from major metropolitan areas into remotely located small towns and cities.

Preparation of the nation's society to meet the demands of the knowledge age became a top priority by the year 2000. This priority fueled changes in the educational environment. The importance of knowledge-based systems to improve and sustain competitive advantage was recognized. The learning model shifted from skills education to knowledge education. Thus, the recognition and acceptance of the need for change and the implementation of change have brought the nation to an enviable position in the year 2010 as the world's economic leader. Dare the nation fall from the position it has worked so diligently to reach? Indeed, no! The nation must work to maintain its position and reach new heights with continual improvement in the standard of living and in the quality of life.

Does this scenario characterize the nation in which you would like to live in the year 2010? Yes, indeed! To make this scenario become a reality, the environments from which the nation must respond include the business environment, the knowledge systems environment, and the education environment.

Preparing for the future is a three-fold endeavor. First, the past must be studied. Second, the activities in the present should reflect the knowledge gained from the past. And, third, these experiences must be continually evaluated. These past and present experiences should be reflected by changes in the economic, societal, and learning models. Model development must be an iterative process; and corresponding changes in the business, knowledge systems, and educational environments must be reflected in these iterations.

The challenge before the nation is great. The alternative, to allow others to shape the nation's destiny, is not acceptable. But what are the challenges that lie ahead in terms of the business, knowledge systems, and education environments?

BUSINESS ENVIRONMENT

Recognition of the need to improve productivity to meet the demands of a global business environment and the development of resources to do so are imperative. An understanding of the fact that the formulas for improving productivity and the quality of goods and services that were used in the past decade are not sufficiently robust for today or for the future is a must. Improving productivity requires greater synergy and integration among the components of productivity and among the business and education sectors. Keys to productivity today include people, capital investment, and technological advancements.

People, the ultimate key to the improvement and continuation of the nation's culture, must be empowered with knowledge assets; capital

33

investments must increase; and advances in technology must continue. For these keys to productivity to be nurtured, informed change must become the nation's byword. Informed change requires that decision makers employ the scientific method of decision making before rendering decisions and attempting to implement changes.

The structure of organizations and work, knowledge development and knowledge management methods, and personnel leadership practices must be altered. These changes have the potential of providing direction and focus for the productivity improvement of workers.

Organizational and work structure. The organizational structure, characterized in the past as hierarchical, must move from the matrix structure of the present to a cluster/collaborative structure. The cluster/collaborative structure will allow individuals to join together to solve business problems. Clusters will be formed as the situation requires and then be disbanded when the project has been completed. Members of a cluster need not be in the same geographic location but will come together to solve a business problem aided by telecommunications networks.

A database system comprised of a skills inventory of employees will facilitate bringing together individuals with complementary skills to form a cluster for the purpose of solving a specific problem or working on a particular project. The organizational environment that fosters this changing work structure will need to provide challenging jobs, appropriate tools, and the latitude to accomplish the goals required by the projects.

Knowledge development and management. Management of knowledge within the clusters will be a nontrivial pursuit; it will be significantly aided by technologically based systems. These systems are commonly called knowledge-based systems. Knowledge-based systems are computer systems designed to provide users with counsel to facilitate decision making. This advice might be viewed on a competency continuum ranging from intelligent assistance in limited problem domains to assistance equal to or exceeding the proficiency of human experts. Knowledge-based systems include an array of systems such as expert systems, group and cooperative work systems, executive information systems, and electronic mail systems.

What is the technology driving the development of these systems? The answer is in the Intel 80386 microcomputer chip. The introduction of the 80386 microprocessor at the end of 1986 ushered in the third generation of personal computers. This microprocessor has become the industry-standard for PC workstations, stations designed to provide within the user's immediate grasp a powerful array of tools. It is these workstations that are the foundation for the development of the variety of knowledge-based systems that are being introduced today and will continue to be introduced as the nation approaches the year 2010.

The industry 80386-based workstation is the universal workstation of the synergistic knowledge age. These universal workstations give knowedge workers the vehicles for applying technology intelligently. They provide an array of features heretofore beyond their grasp. One of the major features is connectivity. The 80386-based workstations provide access to a variety of information sources including mainframe databases and public and private databases, public and private telecommunications networks to name a few. A second feature is that of compatibility. The 80386-based workstations are touted to be compatible with approximately 18 million installed industry standard PC's. The third feature, which the nation has come to expect with each technological breakthrough, is power. The 80386-based workstations do not let the users down; they provide users with more power than the mainframes of a decade ago. More importantly, the 80386-based workstations give knowledge workers the potential for multitasking, running several programs simultaneously.

Productivity improvement. What, then, do these general purpose workstations mean to the business environment? These workstations have the potential for directing and focusing the productivity of knowledge workers. At the very least, they can be the means for improving the productivity of individuals. More far-reaching is their potential for increasing the productivity of groups, collaboratives, and teams. Networked workstations have the potential for allowing the sharing of resources, including hardware, software, and the communication of information and ideas. Timely sharing of such resources facilitates brainstorming, the synthesis of ideas, and thus, the creativity of work groups as they work toward the formulation of a decision or solution. Improved decision making will be the end result as individuals with a variety of expertise are brought together to apply their expertise. The unique capabilities of each individual are thus available to assist in the decision-making process.

The productivity of work groups will be enhanced through the next generation of applications software. New applications software promises to take advantage of distributed processing and, thus, affords the opportunity for increasing end-user productivity. Distributed processing provides users with access to computing power at three levels: the individual workstation or node, the network server, and the mainframe. Through the concept of distributed processing, applications software might use the computing power of more than one microprocessor; the front end on a node or workstation might handle some processing while a back end on the network server or mainframe might handle other processing tasks.

Today decision making by groups of knowledge workers is facilitated by applications software that is available on minicomputer office automation systems and that is downloaded to microcomputer systems. By the year 2000, decision making will be facilitated by the networking of the universal workstations, the sharing of applications software and peripherals, and by the preparation of knowledge workers and other users to understand and to utilize the capabilities of technology.

Personnel leadership. The implementation of the cluster structure in organizations, enhanced by the universal workstations, will require new personnel management practices. Indeed, organizations will refer to such practices as personnel leadership practices. Policies and procedures for reporting, controlling, and evaluating are yet uncharted. Reporting policies may dictate that the project/group leader be responsible and accountable for the group for the duration of a given project. Since group membership will be dictated by the expertise needed for a given project, project leadership will be fluid, changing as does the group organization.

Control policies and procedures will be minimized to encourage creativity and innovation in making decisions and/or arriving at solutions. Groups will be given the tools to do the job, the freedom to be creative, and ample latitude to achieve goals.

Evaluation of personnel will be contingent upon the results of the effort of a cluster/group on a given project. Peer evaluation may also play a role. Thus, the traditional compensation models will begin to wane in favor of compensation based on the accomplishment of specific objectives agreed upon by the group members at the commencement of the project.

Given the cluster organizational structure, the universal workstation, and a work environment encouraging and fostering creativity, innovation, and experimentation, the human element will need to be equipped to work efficiently and effectively if increased productivity, the key to economic development, is to prevail.

Knowledge workers will need to master the four C's: communication, comprehension, critical thinking, and copying. The dynamics of the work-group structure will place a heavy emphasis on speaking and listening ability. Comprehension will require the ability to understand fully the dynamics of the work environment and the many facets of the problem and/or project being investigated. Critical thinking skills will be needed to evaluate various alternatives to problem solution. Coping skills will be needed to deal with the changing technology and the changing group dynamics as groups disband upon completion of a project and new groups are formed.

KNOWLEDGE SYSTEMS ENVIRONMENT

Knowledge workers equipped with the four C's, communication skills, comprehension skills, critical thinking skills, and coping skills, should be well prepared for the knowledge systems environment since it overlaps with the business environment. Knowledge-based systems can be defined as a group of interrelated, interdependent elements joined together for the express purpose of imparting or sharing knowledge. Knowledge-based systems applications are said to be the key to economic development. Knowledge-based systems in the business environment provide knowledge to assist in the management of the organization. Knowledge about organizational management has been coined organizational knowledge. Today, such knowledge is resident in the organization's documents and the organization's leaders. The challenge is to capture, manage, and share this knowledge with members of the organization as needed in the decision-making process to facilitate the achievement of the organization's goals.

Knowledge exists in two forms. Declarative knowledge is factual knowledge and is represented by data. Procedural knowledge is process knowledge. Both declarative knowledge and procedural knowledge are important in generating organizational knowledge. This organizational knowledge has the potential for increasing the productivity of knowledge workers and, thus, can enhance competitive advantage.

Knowledge-based systems have as their foundation information systems. Information systems provide data for decision making; knowledge-based systems build upon that data; they provide knowledge about how to interpret the data. The evolution of computerized processing might be envisioned along a continuum with electronic data processing at one end of the continuum and knowledge processing at the other end of the continuum. A variety of systems have evolved to facilitate the processing of data, information, and knowledge in organizations at the various points along the continuum.

As the economy of the United States continues to move from an industrial base to a service base, the number of knowledge-oriented professions will grow. These knowledge-oriented professions will require knowledge-based systems. The development of knowledge-based systems will require individuals who understand the components of knowledge work.

Knowledge work. Knowledge work requires knowledge acquisition, knowledge representation, and knowledge utilization. Knowledge acquisition is the process of gathering that knowledge and encoding the knowledge into a computer-based system. Given that the knowledge in business organizations is often a composite of knowledge from several sources and may not be certain knowledge, acquiring this knowledge is a complex problem. Also, the difference between expertise and an expert must be understood if the appropriate knowledge is to be gathered. Expertise is the ability to perform a given function or task; it can be acquired through practice. A human expert is an individual who is able to solve difficult, unstructured problems that he or she has never encountered in the past.

Understanding the relationships between the knowledges gathered is important if these relationships are to be gathered and stored in the computer system. For example, understanding the relationship between a profit center's advertising budget and sales is complex. While sales may be influenced by dollars expended for advertising, there may be many other intervening variables in the business environment that are influencing sales.

The second component of knowledge work is knowledge representation. How might knowledge be best represented and stored in a computer system? Some of the approaches in use include representing knowledge by rules or frames. The level at which knowledge should be represented also requires some thought. (For example, knowledge is often viewed at two levels, surface knowledge and deep knowledge.)

The third component of knowledge work, knowledge utilization, is a precarious one for business organizations. Decisions that are made based on the use of knowledge-based systems must be made in light of the fact that a business knowledge-based system by virtue of its subject area may not be able to generate knowledge or counsel that can be guaranteed to be 100 percent infallible. The fact that uncertainties exist in the business problem domain causes some consternation in accepting the counsel of knowledge systems. However, knowledge-based systems are being developed that report a confidence level for the counsel being generated, much as is done in reporting statistical results from research.

Knowledge engineering. Knowledge engineering is the branch of artificial intelligence concerned with designing and developing knowledge-based systems. In particular, knowledge engineering has been concerned with developing expert systems in the last decade. While expert systems development has been the purview of knowledge engineering, expert systems are but one type of knowledge-based system. Given the importance of generating knowledge-based systems in the subject area of business to increase productivity of knowledge workers and others and, thus, improve competitive advantage, it is imperative that knowledge workers and other workers understand the potential of such systems, be able to use them to the fullest extent possible, and be able to help in the generation of such systems. To do so, the educational environment becomes critical.

EDUCATIONAL ENVIRONMENT

Given the paradigm shifts in the economy, in society, and in the development of knowledge-based systems, the educational community becomes a significant player in both the reeducation and education of individuals for the knowledge age. The business education community in particular must be a dynamic force in the reeducation and education of people for the knowledge age. The role of business education—preparation of people with knowledges, skills, and attitudes for and about business—need not change; the importance of the role of business education need not change. However, the implementation of the role *must* change.

Role of business education. The business education community is indeed responsible for the education of knowledge workers in particular and for the education of people about business in the knowledge age. The implementation of the role of business education must reflect the changes in the economy, in society, and in the development of knowledge-based systems. Knowledge is power in the economy of the knowledge age and, thus, the premier resource for the production of wealth. Given the importance of knowledge-based systems to economic development, the business education community must prepare people as intelligent users of knowledge-based systems, as developers of these systems, and as assistants to systems developers. Given the increasing cultural diversity within the United States as well as the need to compete in a global business environment, it becomes imminent that the nation's business education environments provide students with cultural literacy and language literacy. Understanding the mores of the country in which business is being transacted and understanding the subtleties of the business language becomes very important if business graduates are to be efficient and effective in transacting business in multinational business and in multiple countries.

In addition to changes in the economic model and the development of knowledge-based systems impacting the direction and focus for business education, the role and implementation of business education must be influenced by the changing population demographics. Some of these demographic changes include the population aging, ethnic diversity, and geographic dispersion.

Implementation of the role of business education, thus, requires business educators to account for changes in systems, in the economy, and in society in the development of business education learning models.

Knowledge engineering process model. The knowledge engineering process model used in the development of expert systems might prove useful in developing business education learning models and strategies for the preparation of students to meet the demands of the information age. The knowledge engineering process model requires that the knowledge needed by the computer system be captured, that the knowledge be represented in the computer's knowledge base, that software be designed to enable the computer to make inferences based on the knowledge, and that a line of reasoning be designed and programmed into the computer system. In recent years knowledge engineers, who are characterized as self-learners, quick, and analytical, have used this model effectively to develop expert systems.

Business education students, too, must become knowledge engineers. They, too, must be self-learners, quick, and analytical if they are to be prepared to function in the knowledge age. Some business education graduates will be users of these knowledge-based systems called expert systems; other business education graduates will become developers of business knowledge-based systems; still others will assist in the development of business knowledge-based systems. The knowledge engineering process model used to develop expert systems can provide business graduates with a framework for developing business knowledge-based systems.

Business education learning model. The knowledge engineering process model may also be a model for learning for business education students. In knowledge-based systems declarative knowledge is separated from procedural knowledge. This separation facilitates the maintenance of knowledge-based systems. Knowledge-based systems can, thus, be updated more easily by modifying or inserting new declarative knowledge or procedural knowledge. However, a knowledge-based system also has an inference engine designed to help the computer make inferences based on the declarative and procedural knowledge.

Business education students must also be able to make inferences based on knowledge. Thus, business education learning environments also must provide the integration of both declarative and procedural knowledge and the integration of knowledge with concepts and theories. Such integration will help stimulate idea generation and creativity in students. Teaching facts or skills along with applications of those facts or skills is imperative. This procedure can facilitate the transferability of what is learned in the classroom to the job situation. For example, in conjunction with teaching the skills required to use a particular software package, the skills can be practiced by using business cases that provide students with the context within which the skills will be used in business and, thus, with concepts from specific business disciplines. The lament of one executive recently was that today's graduates don't realize that when they enter the business environment, problems to be solved will not necessarily be handed to them as problems; rather the employee must, first, be able to recognize that a problem exists; second, be able to determine what the problem is; and third, be able to formulate the problem before working toward problem solution. Thus, the educational environment must be prepared to provide students with a model for learning that will take them through all phases of problem solving, including problem recognition and problem identification, and is transferable outside the school environment.

The implementation of business education learning models requires that population demographics be carefully considered.

DEMOGRAPHICS. The aging of the population suggests that more people seeking education beyond high school will have had a significant amount of work experience. Thus, business education will need to provide for the reeducation of the population. These experienced, mature students are more likely to demand rigor and relevance in what they are taught. Classroom delivery methods need to reflect the variety of learning resources available including the students themselves who bring a diverse set of experiences to the classroom.

Another demographic change that will significantly influence the direction and focus of business education is the increasing ethnic diversity of the U.S. population. The United States is indeed becoming a microcosm of the world. This ethnic diversity fosters the need for cultural literacy, business language literacy, and cultural values literacy. Business education has a significant role to play in providing business ethics education to facilitate the conduct of business in a pluralistic cultural society.

Yet another demographic change that is beginning to impact the educational environment is the geographic dispersion of the population. As people relocate outside metropolitan areas, the reeducation market requires varied delivery methods. Many of these delivery methods are already being used to supplement the traditional structured institutional classroom approach to instructional delivery. These methods include distributed classrooms facilitated by telecommunication networks, remote learning via electronic media, video presentations, and multimedia presentations by more than one instructor to name a few.

DELIVERY SYSTEMS. The nation must reexamine the impact of its educational delivery systems at all levels of business education. Thoughtful decisions must be made about what learning should take place in traditional educational institutions and what learning is better conducted in other locations. For a number of years the cooperative education delivery method has been successful in providing a joint business/education delivery system. With advances in technology and the fundamental changes in the way work is performed making it difficult for the educational environment to respond in a timely fashion to the needs of the business environment, variations of cooperative education as we know it today will be desirable. Business firms and educational institutions should join together in the education of personnel and in the development of products and services and, thus, expedite the rate of technology transfer. An example of cooperative efforts can be illustrated by recent efforts of American Telephone and Telegraph Company (AT&T), International Business Machines Corporation (IBM), and Massachusetts Institute of Technology (MIT). These three entities have joined together for the purpose of exploring the potential for commercial applications of superconductors. While laser disk and video technologies were developed in the United States, Japan is profiting from the commercialization of these technologies. The joint venture of AT&T, IBM, and MIT is a synergistic effort between business and education to increase the rate at which new products and services are developed from existing technology and ideas, and thus improve the productivity and competitive advantage of the United States.

EVALUATION METHODS. Methods for assessing or evaluating learning must reflect the changing evaluation methods in the business environment given the changing structure in organizations. Some of these methods include projects, performance tests, and case studies. The outcome of evaluation processes must be further development of individuals, not punitive measures, if the nation does indeed believe that people, not pieces of equipment, are the most important ingredient in its economic development.

SYNERGISM. Because of changes in the business environment and the knowledge environment, the education environment finds itself in a dynamic state. The linkages among the business environment, the knowledge systems environment, and the education environment must be more than links in a chain intertwined or joined at some point. An integration of the three environments must occur at many points, and synergism must be the end result.

The knowledge-based systems development process has as its key components people from the educational environment, the knowledge-based systems, and the business environment. Representatives from these three environments need to work cooperatively if people are to be prepared for occupations in the knowledge age. People need to be educated in knowledge systems competencies, knowledge-based systems need to be built by individuals, and the systems need to be used in the business environment where they can then be further modified and refined by people as needed.

One catalyst for stimulating the synergistic efforts of these three environments might be the formation of corporate advisory boards for educational institutions. The purpose of the corporate advisory board would be to facilitate cooperative teaching and learning programs for educators, students, and business personnel and to advise schools about their programs and curriculum. Since futurists predict the nation's businesses will move toward the need for industry specialists rather than functional specialists, representatives on this board should come from the various businesses, from manufacturing industries, from government agencies, and from education. The representatives would need to be individuals whose education and/or work background and experiences are in a variety of disciplines. These disciplines should include not only the business disciplines but also the liberal arts and humanities disciplines as well. This broad range of representation is imperative since businesses are requiring the need for industry specialists with the shift in economic models.

SUMMARY

How, what, when, and where people learn and how, what, when, and where they are taught must indeed be functions of the synergism among the economic, societal, and knowledge-based systems' environments. More important, the boundaries of the United States must not define the boundaries of the economic, business, and education environments.

Learning how to learn and becoming a creative, lifelong learner must become goals of education in the knowledge age or age of synergism. Knowledge is changing too rapidly to expect that formal education can provide all one must know to function in one's work careers. Developing higher order thinking skills needed to solve unstructured problems and to facilitate the use and development of business knowledge-based systems is imperative if the nation is to regain its leadership position in the world economy.

If business education students are to be successful in learning how to learn and in developing critical thinking skills, the educational environment must focus on their strengths. Students must have the opportunity to excel if they are to be motivated to greater achievements. The Greek biographer and historian Plutarch stated that if learners are to learn they must have the opportunity to achieve. This message is as important today as it was in the first century of the Christian era.

Addressing the challenges before the nation in terms of the business, the knowledge systems, and the education environments is not an easy task but a rewarding one. Through the synergism created by people working together within these environments the scenario of the United States as the world's economic leader in the year 2010 will become a reality.

CHAPTER 5

Developing Business Skills Needed in the 1990's

WILMA JEAN ALEXANDER
Illinois State University, Normal

LONNIE ECHTERNACHT
University of Missouri-Columbia, Columbia

The challenges facing business educators are exciting as the year 2000 approaches. The basic concepts of business in many cases remain the same, but the tools to be applied to those concepts have changed and will continue to change at an exponential rate.

The Bureau of Labor Statistics reported in 1988 that the demand for individuals with business skills will continue beyond the year 2000. General clerical workers, secretaries, receptionists, information clerks, clerical supervisors, and managers are job classifications included in the job grouping that will account for one-half of the total job growth between the years 1986-2000. In contrast, the fields of stenography, statistical clerks, typists, and word processors will show a percentage decline. Even though some occupational clusters will show an overall percentage decline, the jobs within some industries will grow at the same pace as total employment. For example, secretaries will expand at the same pace as total employment in personnel supply services, offices of physicians, and legal services; whereas, moderate decreases can be expected in other industries.

LEVELS OF INSTRUCTION

Business and its effects are experienced by all individuals within society. It is important that business educators assist in the development of curriculums that create an awareness of and interest in business. The teaching of concepts for and about business must begin in kindergarten and continue through the senior citizens level. Critical questions which must be addressed include: What are we doing to influence the elementary curriculum? What should we be doing? What is the appropriate approach?

An awareness of business and its role in a democratic society should begin at an early age. Business educators must exercise the initiative to identify concepts that need to be learned if children are to develop into effective contributors to and consumers of goods and services.

Awareness. An awareness of business helps to generate an interest and fosters continued learning on the part of students. Such learning results in opportunities for students to apply knowledge and skills being learned to their everyday challenges. Business education classes can provide opportunities for students to learn effective living skills and to become better consumers and investors. Developing these skills ultimately helps to expand the economy and raise the standard of living.

Entry-level skills. As students recognize the importance of preparing themselves to earn a living, it is imperative that business education programs be relevant and appropriately reflect those skills which are required in the workplace. Entry-level skill requirements are increasing due to new technologies, participative management, sophisticated statistical quality controls, increased emphasis on customer services, and the movement toward just-in-time production.

Workplace basics. Entry-level technical skills are important for initial employment in the workplace. But to be successful and remain successful students must acquire not only technical skills but also "workplace basics" as identified in an interim report, "Workplace Basics: The Skills Employers Want."[1] Seven skill groups were identified:

1. Learning to read
2. 3 R's (reading, writing, computation)
3. Communication: listening and oral
4. Creative thinking/problem solving
5. Self-esteem/goal setting/motivation/personal and career development
6. Interpersonal/negotiation/teamwork
7. Organizational effectiveness/leadership.

Such skills must be taught not in theory only but in a workplace context. Placing these skills in a workplace context enables students to apply and expand the use of the concepts to actual job performance.

Lifelong learning. Training does not and will not end with formal education. Individuals must be able to acquire new as well as more sophisticated technical skills as the workplace changes and new demands are placed on workers.

INSTRUCTIONAL PROGRAMS

Learning styles. Not all students learn the same way. Some can comprehend by reading only, others require exercising other senses, such as hearing, feeling, touching, tasting, or a combination of the options. For some students it may be necessary to provide assistance. Assistance might include a copy of lecture notes or a detailed outline of the lecture. Some students would find it helpful if teachers formulated chapter notes with an accompanying list of terms to be defined. Copies of transparencies could be distributed to the students for future reference. When giving writing assignments to students, provide examples that show intended outcomes. To foster teamwork skills, use group exercises which lead to a cooperative writing assignment based

---

[1]Carnevale, Anthony; Gainer, Leila J.; and Meltzer, Ann S. *Workplace Basics: The Skills Employers Want, Interim Report.* Washington, D.C.: U.S. Department of Labor, 1988.

on group consensus. As business increases its emphasis on teamwork, group projects become more important. Group projects might include doing research, arranging for a guest speaker, developing solutions to case studies, creating visuals, and making presentations.[2] Learning to work together for the mutual benefit of all will assist in developing a favorable work ethic— a work ethic which is needed if U.S. employers are to remain on the competitive edge.

Competency-based learning. When identifying what competencies should be taught and the level of performance to be achieved, a sincere effort must be made to determine the jobs for which students are being prepared, the tasks required for each job classification, and the level of competence required for job entry as well as for advancement on the job. Instructional materials and activities should be developed that will prepare students to perform at an acceptable level.

Transfer of learning. "Transfer refers to the effect that learning one kind of material or skill has on the ability to learn something new."[3] To prepare students for the twenty-first century, developing transferable skills and understandings which can be applied to rapidly changing situations must be emphasized. The major goal will be to provide appropriate instruction that leads to lifelong learning and focuses on decision making as well as adapting to change.

There are two types of transfer. Horizontal transfer refers to a situation in which the skill learned in training can be applied directly to the worksite to solve a problem. In contrast, vertical transfer requires that new learning occur before the skill learned can be adapted to the workplace to solve a problem.

To assist students in developing the ability to transfer skills learned in one situation to others, the following procedure is recommended:

1. Present the theory of the skill through presentations, demonstrations, reading assignments, etc. It is important that students understand the rationale behind the skill, how the skill is used in the workplace, and the rules that govern its use.

2. Demonstrate the skill through simulation, films, videotapes, or ideally, experimentally.

3. Practice the skill under conditions that closely approximate the workplace.

4. Provide feedback about performance. Feedback can be created by supervisors, peers, and self-evaluations.

The real impact on students' perceptions is in the way we teach knowledge, not the knowledge itself. Students must not only master knowledge but they must also master strategies for using that information in relation to specific problems they encounter.

Articulation. Curriculum must be developed and implemented which provides sequential learning experiences for students. The National Business

---

[2]Bartelheim, Frederich J. "Instructional Interventions for Special Needs Students." *Business Education Forum* 43:3-4; January 1989

[3]Joyce, Bruce R., and Clift, Renee Tipton. "Teacher Education and the Social Context of the Workplace." *Childhood Education* 61:115-27; November/December 1984.

Education Association has published an articulated curriculum guide for K-14. The guide is an excellent source of information for planning an articulated curriculum in local school districts as well as within states. The guide, *Database of Competencies for Business Curriculum Development, K-14*, is available from the National Business Education Association.

Articulation of business education curriculum insures a smooth transition for students, provides continuity in the educational process, and contributes to efficient use of resources as students progress through the different levels of education. Articulation can be facilitated through activities such as meetings with the affected parties; teacher exchange programs; achievement testing; sharing of equipment, facilities, and materials; advisory councils; a team approach to the development of one- and five-year plans; and transition committees composed of teachers from local schools and teacher education institutions.

Another curriculum development effort designed to foster articulation is the *Office Opportunities Model Curriculum for Secondary Business Education* which is available from Professional Secretaries International, 301 Armour Boulevard, Suite 200, Kansas City, Missouri 64111-1299. Also, the Data Processing Management Association, 505 Busse Highway, Park Ridge, Illinois 60068-3191 has prepared three curriculum guides: one for high schools, one for community colleges, and one for four-year institutions.

Experiential learning. If students are to understand, it is important that they have the opportunity to "learn by doing them" as stated by Aristotle in his opening chapter of *Nicomachean Ethics.* The Chinese proverb "I do and I understand" is often minimized in the educational environment. We must increase students' active involvement in the learning process if they are to take responsibility for their own learning. Engaging in group activities, speaking before other members of the class, and having opportunities to define their own intellectual positions provide students with opportunities to develop skills that lead to success in the workplace. Through experiential education students can apply knowledge gained vicariously in the classroom and develop action-oriented skills.

Business skills required for the 1990's will include both basic skills, which are required of all workers, and job specific skills. Only as workers understand the environment in which the decisions are to be made can they effectively apply the tools to develop solutions to problems.

KEYBOARDING

Keyboarding, the entering of alphabetic and numeric data, is central to information processing. Even though voice-activated machines are available and will be more readily available in the future, it is predicted that they will be too costly for most offices to acquire. Therefore, to increase productivity and make maximum use of available time, it is imperative that all students develop keyboarding skill.

The skill should be taught when it is required to achieve program goals through frequent and repeated use of the keyboard. If students are using the keyboard for entry of one-key responses, it is not necessary. However, when students begin using the keyboard for writing and programming, correct keyboarding techniques should be taught to prevent the development of bad habits.

It is recommended that the keyboarding teacher be actively involved in the teaching-learning process. Keyboarding software may be used but it should be supplemented with demonstrations as well as close monitoring, supervision, and evaluation of the class. Sufficient time must be allowed to develop automatic responses. If students are to maintain the keyboarding skills learned, they must have frequent access to computers for writing assignments. Teachers must continually monitor and encourage students to use appropriate techniques.

Related keyboarding skills taught should be based on job demands. Teachers must modify curriculums based on the career aspirations of class members. More emphasis should be placed on keyboarding from rough-draft materials for those aspiring to enter the secretarial profession than for those aspiring to be managers. Managers tend to use computers more for inputting alphabetic and numeric data, storing data, retrieving data, communicating with others, and correcting errors using both "backspace" and "type over." Managers are involved to a lesser degree in keying from rough drafts, interoffice memorandums, and vertical and horizontal centering.

Rate of reading. If students attempt to read at their normal reading level when keyboarding, errors will occur. Students must be taught to adjust their normal reading rate downward. This will only occur when a conscious effort is made by the student with the help of the instructor through proper instruction, motivation, and reinforcement. The way copy is read will be based in part on the keyboarding skill of the individual student.

Teach to think. Keyboarding can be used as an avenue to teach thinking according to Scaglione.[4] After the keyboard has been introduced, the following methods are suggested to develop "thinking" skills:

1. Call a word such as "light." Have students respond with an opposite such as "dark."
2. Call list of words. Give students time to key, proofread, and correct errors. Students might also be required to create sentences using the words from the list dictated.
3. Using different letters of the alphabet, have students create word lists beginning with a specific letter.
4. Call out a word, have students respond with words that rhyme.

Since teaching students to think is considered one of the basic skills of the workplace, teachers should create opportunities to develop basic thinking skills as well as creative thinking skills when case problems are being examined.

---

[4]Scaglione, Janet. "To Key or Not to Key . . . That Is the Question." *Business Education Forum* 43:11-12; February 1989.

WORD PROCESSING

The demand for word processors is expected to increase but is not expected to offset the decreased demand for typists. However, word processing should not be considered as a tool only for secretaries and word processors but as a tool for all office workers. As a tool, many teachers are experiencing the integration of word processing into the English, communications, graphics, data processing, and science curriculums. For business education to have a specific niche in the educational field it is necessary to expand word processing into information management. Information management includes not only the inputting, formatting, and outputting of information but also the planning, designing, controlling, and coordination of the communication processes through advanced technology.[5]

The major objectives of word processing are to improve the quality and accuracy of information, to increase the speed of distributing information, and to achieve greater communication economy. To achieve these objectives students must not only be taught keyboarding and word processing but also database management, calendaring, spreadsheets, graphics, and tele-communications.

Word processing functions taught should include how to create, edit, and save a document; sort lines or groups of lines; search (find) specific text; draw lines; and transfer files between different software and hardware. Students should be introduced to the use of compatible software programs such as a spell checker, thesaurus, outline tool, and grammar checker that can be used with word processing programs.

Other concepts that should be included in word processing instruction include booting up, retrieving documents, moving the cursor, deleting characters, transposing characters, inserting/typeover, exiting the document, changing menu defaults, printing, and quitting the program. Setting margins, setting and using tabs, and centering can be introduced when presenting modified block letter style with indented paragraphs. Additional functions that should be taught include boldfacing, caps lock, and underlining.

When presenting the business report format, present the new format, block deletion, moving text, page breaks, searching, and searching and replacing. The use of the function keys as well as how to proofread and change the format of a document are important components to be taught in word processing. It should be emphasized that word processing instruction should include not only the use of software and hardware but also proper interaction with people based on planned procedures.

COMPUTER OPERATION

Today the personal computer (PC) is a fixture in most business organizations, large and small. However, the PC itself is constantly evolving.

---

[5]Lundgren, Terry D. "Word Processing as Information Management." *Journal of Education for Business* 64:327-29; April 1988.

Frequently, a new model is marketed which has substantially more power and capabilities than the previous model and is smaller in size.

Since the disk operating system (DOS) is the vehicle used to communicate with the computer, students must become familiar with its functions. Without DOS, a user would need a degree in computer science to operate the microcomputer. DOS functions include loading a program in the proper location in RAM; accessing data from the proper file; storing data in secondary storage; deleting files; updating the status of which files are stored in which sectors by changing the file allocation table; and selecting, interpreting, and issuing commands to the computer for execution.

File, time, and disk commands should be taught. File commands such as COPY, DIR, ERASE, RENAME, and TYPE should be included. The fundamental time commands are DATE and TIME. These file and time commands are internal commands and are executed immediately since they are built into the command processor.

Disk commands are external and must be read into the computer to be executed. They are stored in separate files and are often referred to as utility files. Examples of disk commands include CHKDSK, DISKCOPY, and FORMAT.

In addition to the DOS commands, students should be introduced to naming files, maintaining files, and security measures. Students should be acquainted with hard disk directory systems as well as storing files, designing subdirectories, and managing directories on a hard disk system.

Lone and Blaskovias recommended that computer operations should be taught through a hands-on approach using interdisciplinary applications which are problem oriented.[6] Since the major computer in use by businesses today is IBM or IBM compatible, it is recommended that business education use what is used in business.

Instruction should include problem-solving techniques as well as problem-solving design. Concepts should be taught as part of the overall management information systems concept rather than as isolated problems. Programming should be limited to an overview of BASIC to develop a logical approach to problem solving and to help students understand how communication occurs between the user and the computer.

An attempt should be made to assist students in interpreting computer operator manuals. Concepts taught should apply to all computer systems including software and hardware. One method found to be very successful is to step students through the learning process of a specific software program, for example, Wordstar. Once they are familiar with that program, assign them a different word processing program to learn without step-by-step guidance. Students then prepare a handout and instruct the class on the use of the new software. This experience prepares students to adapt quickly to new software.

---

[6]Lone, Michael S., and Blaskovias, Thomas L. "Microcomputer Education: An Integrated Approach to Curriculum Design." *Journal of Education for Business* 64:358-62; May 1988.

DATABASE/INFORMATION MANAGEMENT

Office support positions make up one of the largest occupations in the U.S. economy. One area within user support is information management. The knowledge base for information management includes management concepts such as planning, organizing, staffing, directing, and controlling. In addition, systems concepts must be taught, including the relationships and the interaction of those systems to generate information needed for a firm to have a competitive advantage.

The largest media component of an information system is paper. Estimated yearly costs of storing records in a 4-drawer file cabinet varies from $50-$272 based on cost per square foot for the space occupied. The average cost of an MIS file is $60. Users and information specialists must learn the rules and procedures related to information management if information is to be available to the right person, in the right place, at the right time, and at the lowest possible cost.

Theories, principles, rules, laws, and procedures must be presented for all phases of the records cycle from creation through disposition. Word processing, data processing, audio and video recording, optical disks, micrographics, computer output microfilm, computer-assisted retrieval, and telecommunications, as well as the technology associated with each, must be presented if students are to understand the overall concepts of information management. Methods which can be used in teaching information management concepts include lecture, texts, guest speakers, films, journal articles, case studies, simulations, field surveys, company tours, computer simulations, vendor literature, and tours.

SPREADSHEETS/RECORDKEEPING

A spreadsheet program transforms a computer into a "number-crunching" tool capable of solving problems once tackled with a pencil, columnar paper, and a calculator. Spreadsheet programs are useful in organizing data that is normally displayed in rows and columns. Spreadsheets can be employed to organize and experiment with data required to solve a variety of problems—recordkeeping, financial statements, budgets, projections, and "what if" analyses.

Students need to be familiar with spreadsheet templates—reusable worksheets with built-in titles and formulas that guide how the data is processed but do not contain the data. Spreadsheet templates are usually designed by a person who is knowledgeable about spreadsheets and the task to be done and who tries to make the spreadsheet useful to people who know little about either the spreadsheet or the necessary calculations.

Unlike other types of personal computer software that have become segmented into different levels of capabilities to accommodate users' varying expertise, most companies have standardized on a single spreadsheet program for all their spreadsheet users. A general rule of thumb is that it takes 40 hours of reading, practice, experimentation, and mistakes before a person feels proficient with most of the advanced features of a spreadsheet; however, it should take no more than an hour or two to being building simple financial models.[7] Basic concepts, procedures, and business applications of spreadsheets should be taught to students planning to enter an office career.

COMMUNICATING INFORMATION

Organizations operate on information, and people within these organizations constantly need information to plan, coordinate, execute, and control activities being undertaken. Communication systems are designed to distribute information in a timely manner and in the form needed by the user. For organizations to be able to achieve their goals successfully, everyone must have access to accurate and up-to-date information.

Communicating effectively means saying what you want to say, when you want to say it, in words that are easily understood. Becoming a competent communicator requires knowledge, techniques, common sense, and a willingness to try. Two-way communication is needed for planning, idea sharing, and problem solving. Knowing when to talk and communicating concise ideas in a clear manner are keys to success within any organization.

Why is it so important for office workers to have good oral communication skills? Because knowing that one can speak well helps develop self-assurance. By speaking correctly, a professional image—relaxed but businesslike—can be developed.

To help students meet the goal of successful oral communication, the following techniques should be taught: get to the point quickly, don't tack unnecessary questions onto messages, keep the key points in mind, show self-confidence, don't start out with an apology, avoid cliches and wishy-washy words, don't hesitate to hesitate, don't overstate the case, don't repeat yourself, ask questions, and practice, practice, practice. Students need to be encouraged to practice concise communication.

The ability to ask pertinent questions and provide concise, easy-to-understand information may often be the yardsticks used to judge an employee's competence. Being able to think quickly and verbalize well are skills that students can develop through regular use.

TELEPHONE AND OTHER ELECTRONIC MESSAGING

A large majority of the routine operations within an organization involve telephone contact and verbal communication. The telephone is personal, relatively inexpensive, but difficult to control. Actually, more than half of all phone calls require only one-way information flow; only 25 percent of all phone calls require either an immediate response or dialogue.

The use of voice mail has opened a whole new dimension in the area of communicating. Voice mail combines computer technology and push button telephones. This allows messages to be sent using a telephone key pad rather

---

[7]Sullivan, David R.; Lewis, Theodore G.; and Cook, Curtis R. *Computing Today: Microcomputer Concepts and Applications.* Second edition. Boston: Houghton Mifflin Co., 1988. p. 271.

than a computer keyboard. Business managers and executives are often more comfortable using a telephone than they are using a computer. Voice mail is generally regarded as a major time-saver; however, it does not provide a written record.

A relatively new communication tool that is gaining in popularity is called voice message processing. Voice message processing utilizes a computer disk for the storage of messages. In voice message processing, a user dials the system, enters an identification code or password, and then proceeds to create or receive voice messages. Messages can be replied to immediately by sending a response, saved for a later time, edited before they are sent, or forwarded to one or multiple parties. The advantages of voice message processing are: speaking a message is generally easier than keying it; interruptions are eliminated; work can be scheduled rather than arranged around the ring of the phone; and messages can reflect the sense of urgency, tone, and inflections of the sender's own voice.

Facsimile transmission, commonly referred to as fax, combines scanning and telephone technologies to transfer text and images over telephone lines. Facsimile is a type of electronic mail that delivers an exact copy of a document which may contain text, graphs, charts, and pictures to its destination, on time. Companies who are low-volume users may obtain facsimile service from public fax companies which serve business travelers and businesses.

Students need to recognize the importance of good techniques when using the telephone, voice message processing, and facsimile transmission for communicating ideas. The success of office workers also depends on their ability to provide information via the written word. The written word is often used to make contacts with those outside the organization. Business writing will normally have five broad purposes: to inform, to persuade, to instruct, to transmit, and to personalize. Memos, letters, reports, and directions represent different types of documents by which written information flows. Good writing techniques can be learned; and for most business people, writing is a skill that must be developed if they expect to achieve success in their careers.

REPROGRAPHICS SYSTEMS

Reprographics include copying, electronic printing, and electronic publishing. Copiers are often taken for granted because, like the telephone, they exist everywhere. Students should understand the many special features that modern copiers have: image enlargement and reduction, automatic document handling, duplex printing, document assembly, and image editing.

Many electronic printers are laser printers. They use digital technology for generating an image and are capable of generating higher quality output than traditional printers (dot matrix, daisy wheel, and ink-jet printers) used with computers and word processors. The copy produced by laser printers is clean, professional-looking copy that resembles typeset copy. Laser printers can handle almost any type of image ranging from company logos to scientific equations, graphs, and line art as well as text in different fonts and sizes.

Electronic publishing systems may vary in sophistication from a desktop publishing microcomputer-based system to a professional dedicated work-station or system. A typical desktop publishing system includes layout (page composition) software, a computer system with a laser printer for output, a digitized graphics scanner for input, and related software programs includ-ing word processing, graphics, and clip art that are compatible with the layout program.

Training in desktop publishing should include introduction to and use of software, basics of graphic design, availability and use of art work, and hardware requirements. Software functions such as the integration of text and graphics, identification of fonts, font size control, column width, spacing, placement of graphics, position blocks, and adjustment for page breaks should be presented. The basics of graphic design presented should include layout of document, identification of intended audiences, and isolation of the major objective of the publication.

As organizations become more knowledgeable of what desktop publishing has to offer and what the benefits are, more demands are being made on system functions—networking, enhanced personal computer packages, and the inclusion of layout program features into word processing.

RECORDS MANAGEMENT/STORAGE SYSTEMS

While many people think of records management as only the storage and retrieval of information, records management is designed to organize and control all phases of the life cycle of a record. The life cycle of a record refers to the period from the time a record is created until the record is finally destroyed—creation, communication/distribution, use, storage/maintenance, and final disposition. Company records can take many forms—paper, microforms, and electronic media.

The management of records becomes increasingly complicated as companies begin to integrate several different record systems. Records created on word processing systems are often stored on disks. Records generated by computers are usually stored in those computer systems. Incoming records, such as letters and reports, are often stored in a paper-based system. The ownership and security of information become increasingly complicated when records are automated and made available to a number of individuals. An important factor for students to understand is that the records, or information, of an organization belong to the organization just as other assets belong to the organization.

FUTURE CHALLENGES

Businesses are becoming increasingly dependent on up-to-the-minute technology in order to maintain their competitive positions locally as well as in world markets. Businesses have broadened the goals and uses of office automation not only to include the improved productivity of office workers but also to enhance the performance of executives, managers, and profes-sionals throughout an entire organization.

The education and training of office workers is a major concern. Constant technological advances make it difficult for schools to provide state-of-the-art equipment for training. Business leaders, therefore, point out the need to teach students the basic skills, concepts, and systems that underlie office functions and procedures. An employee who has learned the fundamentals of automated office systems in school should be able to master easily and quickly the new equipment and technologies that invade the modern office.

Job roles are changing with the increased use of computers at work-stations—the professional or manager operates the keyboard to initiate and to retrieve documents while the secretary may update and refine the documents. Middle-level managers now perform many routine tasks, and support staff members perform higher-level data manipulation.

Just as job roles are changing so also must the educational process change to prepare individuals to function in those roles. Business educators must research current labor market requirements, review the present curriculum, follow up graduates to determine the relevancy of the curriculum, and modify the curriculum to reflect current job requirements.

We can do it! We must do it! The future of business education depends on each of us to assume our share of the responsibility.

CHAPTER 6

Developing Basic Business Competency

KENNETH W. BROWN
University of Houston, Houston, Texas
CHARLES R. HOPKINS
University of Minnesota, St. Paul

Society has become increasingly concerned about the education of its citizens. Increasingly, the public school system has come under attack. This is as true for curriculums designed to develop basic skills as it is for curriculums designed to develop occupational skills and knowledge. There are charges that our youth are not developing the basic skills necessary to perform as effective consumers and citizens in an increasingly complex social and economic milieu. The charges continue that students cannot develop the occupational skills necessary to perform effectively as workers since they have not mastered the basic skills of reading, writing, and computing.

According to a recent report, *Workplace Basics: The Skills Employers Want*, "Employer complaints focus on serious deficiencies in areas that include problem solving, personal management, and interpersonal skills. The abilities to conceptualize, organize, and verbalize thoughts, resolve conflicts, and work in teams are increasingly cited as critical."[1] The report identifies, in some specificity, the basic work place skills identified as desired by employers.

So what are the skills—those basic workplace skills—that employers want? They certainly include basic skills associated with formal schooling. But academic skills such as reading, writing, and arithmetic comprise just the tip of the iceberg.

Employers want employees who can learn the particular skills of an available job— who have "learned how to learn."

Employers want employees who will hear the key points that make up a customer's concerns (listening) and who can convey an adequate response (oral communications).

Employers want employees who can think on their feet (problem solving) and who can come up with innovative solutions when needed (creative thinking).

Employers want employees who have pride in themselves and their potential to be successful (self-esteem); who know how to get things done (goal setting/ motivation); and who have some sense of the skills needed to perform well in the workplace (personal and career development).

Employers want employees who can get along with customers; suppliers or co-

---

[1]Carnevale, Anthony P.; Gainer, Leila J.; and Meltzer, Ann S. *Workplace Basics: The Skills Employers Want.* Washington, D.C.: U.S. Department of Labor, Employment and Training Administration, 1989. p. 8.

workers (interpersonal and negotiation skills); who can work with others to achieve a goal (teamwork); who have some sense of where the organization is headed and what they must do to make a contribution (organizational effectiveness); and who can assume responsibility and motivate co-workers when necessary.[2]

It is the authors' position that business education can play a major role in helping to develop workers who have the identified skills. Of even more importance is the fact that we can do this in a context that is meaningful. That context is the business-economic system in which students preform their role as consumers and producers. Actually, this claim is not new. Those of us who have worked in business education for more than a few years know about the dual mission of business education and the types of students who can benefit from our courses and programs. That programs are designed to provide learning opportunities for all students, not just students preparing for careers in business, is a concept that has been presented in several of the policy statements prepared and distributed by the Policies Commission for Business and Economic Education. For example, "This We Believe About the Value of a Business Education," a policy statement issued by the Commission in 1981, states:

> The dual mission of business education—to provide education FOR and ABOUT business—should be promoted in every secondary and postsecondary business education program so that
> a. the vocational objective can be accomplished by providing programs which will prepare people for employment in business or as owners and managers of business enterprises; and
> b. the basic business and economic education objective can be accomplished by providing courses and experiences which will equip students with foundational knowledges about business enterprise, personal economics, money and banking, and the like, while at the same time strengthening their basic reading, writing, mathematical, and interpersonal skills.[3]

It is through foundational business courses that students learn the principles in those areas of business and economics that are essential for all people (workers) regardless of their occupations. It is also through these courses that students develop, in context, those basic workplace skills identified previously. While not stated in behavioral form, students should, as a result of their business foundational studies—

1. Learn the basic principles of economics and gain an understanding of and appreciation for the American economic system.
2. Acquire an understanding of the development of business enterprise in the history of our economy.
3. Become aware of their roles as intelligent consumers of economic goods and services.
4. Develop an understanding of the relationship between responsible democratic government and business enterprise.

---

[2]*Ibid.*

[3]"This We Believe About the Value of a Business Education." Policy Statement No. 29. Reston, VA: Policies Commission for Business and Economic Education, 1981.

5. Acquire an understanding of the functional areas of business (finance, accounting, management, marketing).

6. Develop an adequate command of the foundations of business.

7. Develop an understanding of the related business administration disciplines.[4]

The personal finance/economic education of *all* students has long been a focus area of business education. An emerging area that is being given increasing amounts of attention is that of entrepreneurship education. This increased attention is the result of several factors: hundreds of thousands of small business firms are being created annually; most *new* jobs are created by small business firms; and most business failures are the result of managerial incompetence and inexperience. Fiber (1986) recommends that entrepreneurship education "contain areas of instruction that provide youth with an understanding of the characteristics of entrepreneurs, the nature of small business in American society, business management, marketing strategies, finance and accounting, credit, and networking."[5] Thus, while the business foundations for entrepreneurs are essentially the same as for persons seeking business employment, the emphasis of selected courses may be quite different. That is, the emphasis is not on working in a corporate environment but rather on owning or managing a small business and all of the risks and skills inherent in that environment. This will be discussed in more detail in a later section of this chapter.

Business programs, regardless of educational level, must reflect the environment of the business community. There are a number of ways to achieve this. Integration of business community resources in class activities is, of course, essential. Guest speakers, field trips, and specific student projects that require students to spend time in the business community are common ways of accessing business expertise and bringing it to the classroom. Student organizations can also be used to provide activities which bring businesspersons to the educational setting. Student organizations can also provide opportunities for students to take them outside the classroom—to visit places of business and to interact with business professionals about employer expectations and career opportunities. Cooperative education and intern programs also should be used to provide experience which will integrate business experience with classroom learning. This type of interaction will provide constant contact with and feedback from the business community in terms of curricular needs. Not to be forgotten are advisory committees. Their effective use can provide a formal interaction between business and education. This interaction, too, provides important feedback related to curriculum needs. Advisory committees can be especially effective in determining equipment needs, employment trends, and in assessing graduates' preparedness for employment. Finally, teachers must continue to maintain their personal contacts with business firms in the community. Whether it is through actual employment, consulting activities, or periodic observation

[4]Hopkins, Charles R. "Basic Business Teacher Education Programs" *Revitalization of Basic Business Education.* Twentieth Yearbook. Reston, VA: National Business Education Association, 1982. p. 149.

[5]Fiber, Larry Ray. "Entrepreneurship in the High School Curriculum." *Business Education Forum* 40:27; April 1986.

and interviews, it is essential that business teachers keep current with the local business climate—changing employment needs and qualifications and the technological changes and trends.

In the sections that follow, selected foundational areas of business and economic education and their potential contributions to an educated citizenry will be presented.

ECONOMIC EDUCATION AND PERSONAL BUSINESS

As noted previously, one of the major purposes of business education is to provide education to develop economic understanding and personal economic competence. This is generally accomplished in what is called the broad area of basic business education. According to Ann Scott Daughtrey, "Basic business should aid in developing within an individual . . . (1) the knowledge, skills, abilities, and attitudes that will enable him or her to use sound reasoning in making personal business decisions as a consumer of goods and services . . . (2) A level of economic literacy sufficient to enable the individual to analyze alternatives, to make reasoned judgments and sound decisions, and to take intelligent actions as a citizen in a democratic society."[6] These two goals are often summarized in a much abbreviated statement: to develop economic understanding and personal economic competence. A number of courses taught at the secondary and postsecondary levels devote some or all of their content and activities to the achievement of objectives related to economic understanding and personal economic competence. Such courses often carry such titles as general business, consumer economics, applied economics, personal finance, personal money management, and personal business.

A number of states have developed extensive lists of learner outcomes relative to economic understanding and personal economic competence. The Joint Council on Economic Education also provides such listings. To list all, or even a reasonable sample, of these learner outcomes is beyond the scope of this chapter. However, Calhoun's list of consumer education objectives is similar to other lists of personal economic competence objectives and is included as one sample.[7] Because of the extensiveness of this list, only the general objective for an area is given with the exception of objective 3.

1. The student will recognize the importance of estimating income and expenses, clarifying values and goals, making decisions and financial plans.

2. Students will acquire skills that are necessary to make rational decisions when buying for themselves and for their families.

3. Students will be able to state valid reasons for using credit, to identify the types of credit and compute the cost of credit.
   a. Students will identify the concepts of borrowing and credit will be able to list and evaluate reasons for borrowing or using credit.

---

[6]Daughtrey, Ann Scott; Reston, Robert; and Baker, Robert Lee, Jr. *Basic Business and Economic Education—Learning and Instruction.* Cincinnati: South-Western Publishing Co., 1982. pp. 21-22.

[7]Calhoun, Calfrey C. *Managing the Learning Process.* New edition. Bessemer, AL: Colonial Press, 1986. pp. 496-97.

    b. Students will be able to list and evaluate different sources and types of consumer credit.

    c. Students will be able to determine how much credit costs and how to shop for credit.

    d. The student will be able to identify criteria for establishing a good credit rating and will recognize the procedures for using credit wisely.

4. Students will recognize the need for protecting assets, the types of protection available, and the importance of choosing the type of protection most suited to one's means and needs.

5. Students should develop positive attitudes toward investing their resources as a means to achieve future goals.

6. Students will understand why every citizen must share in the cost of public services by paying taxes.

It is not necessary to maintain a separateness between the economic understanding objectives and the personal economic competence objectives. Fersh suggests that there are numerous ways to help students apply economic understanding to their personal lives, in their personal lives, in their households, and in places of work.[8] Let's look at an example of how this might be done relative to one's personal life. Once having earned an income, students face economic decisions about what to do with that income. Decisions must be made about how much and for what to spend; about how much and in what ways to save and/or invest; and, if necessary, about how much and from whom to borrow. This example provides opportunity to apply such economic tools of analysis as opportunity cost and diminishing return. Based on their economic understanding, students in the workplace better understand how to make the best use of the various factors of production available to them. They also understand the need to increase productivity if economic conditions are to improve.

A discussion of the need for all students to develop economic understanding and personal economic competence as presented here often raises the issues of where in the curriculum this content actually belongs. That is, should business educators be providing it, or is it better delivered through the social science or home economics curriculums? There is enough evidence available to indicate that all three departments have a role in this very important educational program. There is much to do and teachers in each subject have special preparation for delivering parts of the program.

Teaching in the area of economic education and personal business requires that a teacher be creative and imaginative. While excellent textbooks and other print materials are available, it is important to take advantage of the many other resources that are also available. Paramount among these is the local community. Carlock writes:

> Let your entire community also be your textbook—you have a wealth of resources at your fingertips. Rarely does a day go by that the daily newspaper does not have news on some development in consumer affairs. Credit bureaus, banks, savings and loan institutions, radio and television stations, retailers, hospital administrators,

[8]Fersh, George L. "The Need for Economic Understanding." *The Emerging Content and Structure of Business Education.* Eighth Yearbook. Washington, D.C.: National Business Education Association, 1970. pp. 89-95.

real estate agents, judges, business executives, car dealers, stockbrokers, and attorneys are all sources of consumer information. Students must have the opportunity to learn outside the classroom as well as in the classroom; teachers must bring the community to the classroom and the classroom to the community whenever possible.[9]

Teachers to be successful must use a variety of teaching methods and resource materials. Again, the only limit is the teacher's creativity and imagination. In addition to the traditional methods of lectures and class discussion, teachers must elicit active student participation through the use of surveys, shopping projects, library projects, oral and written reports, media (print, films, videocassettes), media projects, and various computer-based software packages. Integrating computer applications in this area is extremely important since the computer is not only an instructional aid for the teacher but also an important new consumer resource. Students need to be introduced to the many changes resulting from the technological advancements and applications of these technological changes taking place in the business community. Electronic funds transfer, instant credit checking and approval, automated teller machines, access to a variety of databases, and electronic shopping are just a few examples that affect students directly in their day-to-day personal business activities.

BUSINESS ORGANIZATION AND MANAGEMENT

Another of the major objectives of business education is the preparation of students for employment as owners and managers of business enterprises. These business enterprises range from large corporations with many employees and several layers of management to the small business with few employees and only one or two management layers. A wide variety of courses are taught at the secondary and postsecondary levels to help students effectively perform in management and ownership roles. Many of the courses at the secondary level are of an introductory or survey nature. Some of the more common courses offered at the secondary level carry titles such as general business, introduction to business, business principles, and business organization and management. It is interesting that at the postsecondary level many of these same titles will appear in the curriculum and are also considered to be introductory or survey courses. But at that level, many applied management courses will also be found. Some of the additional course titles found in postsecondary institutions include principles of management, principles of supervision, small business management, credit management, administrative office management, sales management, records management, personnel management, retail management, credit management, and even pyschology of management. Focus in this chapter will be placed on the business organization/introduction to business and management courses.

One of the most common courses found at both the secondary and postsecondary levels is the introduction to business or business organization course.

[9]Carlock, LeNeta L. "Will Your Students Be Effective Consumers?" *New Directions in Teaching Business.* Twenty-second Yearbook. Reston, VA: National Business Education Association, 1984. p. 60.

It appears that there are two types of introduction to business courses. One type, as presented in the curriculum guides of Minnesota and Wisconsin, is a combination of an introduction to personal finance along with a survey of business organization. A typical course description for this type of an introduction to business might read:

> This offering is designed to help students develop a basic understanding of how business functions in today's society. Instruction may include a study of the free-enterprise system; consumerism; insurance; taxation; banking; credit; investments; personal money management; business terminology; the relationships of government, business, and labor; and career opportunities in business.[10]

As one would expect, the learner outcomes for this type of course are a combination of personal economic competence and economic understandings as described in the section on economic education and personal business. Contrast the description above for a secondary school introduction to business course with that from a community college:

> . . . surveys the wide and complex range of operations which constitute the contemporary United States business scene. The latest business theories, as well as brief historical backgrounds, complete this overview of the way today's business community provides goods and services within the legal, ethical, and economic framework of the United States.[11]

Perhaps use of the same course title for two different types of courses is indicative of the communication and articulation problems we encounter in business education.

Another course found at the secondary and postsecondary levels is business organization and management. The course description from the Wisconsin secondary business education curriculum guide reads:

> This offering is designed to help students understand basic concepts of management and the characteristics, organization, and operation of business as a major sector of the economy. Instruction includes a general overview of American business; forms of business ownership with an emphasis on small-business ownership; management functions; personnel management; labor-management relations; trends in policies, procedures, and philosophies of business management; decision making; public and human relations; and women in nontraditional business occupations.[12]

Learner outcomes for the business organization and management course described in the paragraph above are presented below.

> After completing two semesters of Business Organization and Management, the student should be able to—
> 1. Demonstrate an understanding of economic terminology related to business ownership and management
> 2. Indicate an awareness of the types and degree of government control over business
> 3. Describe the fundamental role of American business in the economy

---

[10]Schlattman, Ronald D. (Project Director) "Introduction to Business." *Wisconsin Business Education Curriculum Guide: Supplement #1.* Eau Claire: University of Wisconsin—Eau Claire, 1986. p. 83.

[11]*Catalog: 1984-85.* Holyoke Community College, Holyoke, MA.

[12]Schlattman, *loc. cit.*

4. Formulate a basic concept of internal organization and the functions of management
5. Classify the types of business ownership available to the American business-person and demonstrate an understanding of the advantages and disadvantages of each type
6. Demonstrate an understanding of the American economic system as a modified free-enterprise system
7. Describe the role of a finance department in a company
8. Describe the role of personnel management in selecting, training, and promoting employees
9. Describe the activities of a purchasing department
10. Demonstrate personal traits necessary for being a successful manager
11. Formulate a basic concept of human relations
12. Demonstrate the need for information services in a small business
13. Construct a plan for company compensation and benefits
14. Describe the function of a production department
15. Describe the importance of labor-management relations
16. Describe the services of a marketing department.[13]

Learner outcomes for a principles of management course taught in the vocational technical institutes (two-year postsecondary) in Minnesota are specified in the following way:

1. Describe management theory/science/practice
2. Identify management skills
3. Describe management concept evolution
4. Identify current management theories
5. Describe current management theories
6. Define management function
7. Describe planning function
8. Describe planning strategies
9. Describe organizing function
10. Describe decentralized management
11. Describe centralized management
12. Explain departmentalization methods
13. Identify organizational style/culture
14. Compare organizational leadership styles
15. Describe business politics
16. Describe power base
17. Describe staffing function
18. Identify management styles
19. Identify managerial testing methods
20. Describe managerial development techniques
21. Describe staffing elements
22. Describe controlling function
23. Identify current control processes
24. Compare control strategies

[13]*Ibid.*, pp. 83-84.

25. Describe popular decision-making models
26. Compare popular decision-making models
27. Describe quality/productivity control methods
28. Compare quality/productivity control methods
29. Describe directing/leading function
30. Identify behavior modification concepts
31. Describe behavior modification concepts
32. Identify worker motivation concepts
33. Compare worker motivation concepts
34. Describe organizational leadership responsibility
35. Describe organizational communication structure
36. Identify current organizational communication processes.[14]

Regardless of the course being taught, it is important to use methods and materials that maintain the linkage between the classroom and the business community. Use of speakers, shadowing, special projects (interviews with managers at different levels in a variety of business firms), and career days are all ways through which students can actively relate to business. Work experience, be it in the form of a cooperative education experience or a more formal internship, is also a profitable way for students to spend time in the workplace learning about management and applying learning gained in their formal classes.

Students should be introduced to and gain competence in using the many computer applications that are available to managers to carry out their jobs. These include, of course, the use of spreadsheets, databases, and graphics programs. In addition, students need to use some of the more specialized programs, or integrated programs, that can be used for tax preparation and planning, payroll, finance application for tracking income and expenses, inventory control, etc.

ENTREPRENEURSHIP

Business educators are often presented with opportunities to enhance their image and make significant contributions to the educational institution in which they reside. Although one such opportunity has been at hand for a number of years, only recently has it caught the attention of authorities in the field. That opportunity is the teaching of entrepreneurship.

If one were to peruse the secondary business education curriculums across the country, very few listings of entrepreneurship or owning and operating a small business would be found. However, a great deal of emphasis has been given the topic in community colleges and universities.

There is a need to bring entrepreneurial skills and knowledges to secondary business education students as well. Historically, education has addressed the needs of our society. Certainly entrepreneurship is a need that should be given a priority in our curriculums. Consider the following from Policy Statement No. 42, "This We Believe About the Role of Business Educators in Teaching Entrepreneurship":

---

[14]Pederson, Kathleen M. (Project Director) "Principles of Management." *Minnesota Post-Secondary Curriculum Guide: Wholesale/Retail Marketing Careers.* St. Paul: Minnesota State Board of Vocational Education, 1988, pp. 203-04.

Entrepreneurial venture is immensely important to the American economy.

- Over 600,000 small businesses are created annually.
- Small businesses have grown in number from 5.4 million in 1954 to more than 15 million in 1987.
- Small businesses comprise 97 percent of the nation's companies.
- By 1990 the small-business sector will be responsible for more than 50 percent of the nation's gross national product.
- More than two-thirds of the entry-level jobs are in small businesses.
- The small business sector employs 56 percent of all employees.
- One of eight persons is self-employed.[15]

There should be little discussion about the need for business educators to become involved in this subject matter area. If business educators do not sit up and take notice, then we can surely expect some other department within our educational institution to fill the need.

Two questions to be addressed here are (1) what entrepreneurial skills and knowledges should be taught, and (2) how best to teach them.

Anderson provides an interesting discussion of an entrepreneurship course in her article, "Teach Entrepreneurship . . . Who, Me? Yes, You!" She believes the entrepreneurship course should achieve three goals and provides six programs for implementation.

Goal 1—Make students aware of entrepreneurship as a career option

Goal 2—Help students understand the basic concepts of entrepreneurship

       Program 1. Is it for you? Assessment of personal potential

       Program 2. How do you start? Types of ownership

       Program 3. Do you know your market? Market analysis

Goal 3—Offer students common-sense guidelines for starting their own business venture

       Program 4. What's your plan? Business planning

       Program 5. What's the bottom line? Financial management

       Program 6. How to keep it going: Managing the business.[16]

Interesting and useful course? You bet! Try it, you'll like it and so will your students. But the important point to remember is that you, as a business educator with background expertise, will be addressing a need that is crying out for attention in our schools.

Another approach in teaching entrepreneurship is to integrate the skills and knowledges into existing courses. In Texas, the essential elements for all vocational programs mandate the inclusion of entrepreneurship instruction. It is felt that many vocational students will exit high school programs and move on to employment in small businesses or small business ownership.

As one examines the needed entrepreneurial learner outcomes, it can be seen that a number are part and parcel of other business offerings. For

[15]"This We Believe About the Role of Business Educators in Teaching Entrepreneurship." Policy Statement No. 42. Reston, VA: Policies Commission for Business Education and Economic Education, 1987.

[16]Anderson, Lois. "Teach Entrepreneurship . . . Who Me? Yes, You!" *Business Education World* 69:9-11; Spring 1989.

example, financial recordkeeping will be taught in recordkeeping or accounting; developing a marketing plan will be taught in marketing education programs; managerial skills will be taught in business organization and management courses, and so on.

Using a strategy of integrating entrepreneurship into existing courses is a very viable option and certainly one most high school business educators may need to consider. Adding another elective course to the curriculum is not a high priority in most schools. If the integration approach is used, the business education faculty should develop a plan that will address the need to bring all skills and knowledges to the attention of most department enrollees.

One of the more interesting aspects of entrepreneurship is the opportunity to involve the business community. Small business owners are highly motivated individuals who have a desire to succeed. They are interested in discussing their accomplishments with students and should be involved in classroom activities whenever possible. Field trips or after-school visitations with small business owners are also excellent opportunities for students to see the positives and negatives of being an entrepreneur.

For some unknown reason, business educators seem to believe co-op programs can only operate within funded vocational education. That need not be the case. Why not arrange afterschool cooperative agreements with small business owners? These individuals usually have a need for help. The exposure students receive in co-op assignments cannot be duplicated in the classroom.

Business teachers should also avail themselves of the information and expertise of the Small Business Administration. This organization was established for the sole purpose of assisting small business owners and can be an excellent resource. Their materials are tried and tested, and their personnel have seen many examples of successful entrepreneurs and those who fail.

The entrepreneurship content provides business educators with an excellent opportunity to integrate computers into the classroom. Software packages are available from the various vendors and have proved to be very helpful in the classroom.

RECORDKEEPING/ACCOUNTING

Those business educators who would like to improve our image by offering more demanding courses usually target recordkeeping as one for elimination. The reading level is low, topics are of a personal nature, and classes are often flooded with underachievers, malcontents, and potential dropouts. However, the course persists for a number of good reasons.

First, our high school population, in far too many instances, has a majority of students who fall within the previously mentioned categories. School counselors and administrators are truly struggling to find enough courses for the unmotivated student to complete for a high school diploma. Second, these students, more than any other group, need the topics found in a general business course, entrepreneurship, or recordkeeping. At least these topics will provide the student with some survival skills.

What should be taught in recordkeeping? The content of a given course text usually dictates the content of a course. Text publishers now find they must meet the curriculum requirements as prescribed by the various state educational agencies, so the content of a given text reflects the collective viewpoints of a number of states. In Texas, for example, the curriculum K-12 is presented in a document entitled "State Board of Education Rules for Curriculum." The requirements for each course are presented via "essential elements." For recordkeeping the major subdivisions of content are (1) recording and maintaining information, (2) banking, (3) money management, (4) payroll, (5) business forms, and (6) processing information electronically.[17]

A common practice of the recordkeeping teachers is to involve the students in practical, hands-on experiences. The recordkeeping enrollees usually learn best by seeing, hearing, and doing. Financial planning practice sets, manual simulations, and computer simulations are appropriate for the recordkeeping student.

If a school has the opportunity, it should offer courses in recordkeeping and accounting. When possible, it is appropriate to schedule the classes at the same time periods throughout the day. This plan provides an opportunity for the business education department to keep the accounting course on an appropriate level. Having both classes scheduled during the same time period permits students having difficulty with accounting to be easily transferred to recordkeeping.

The accounting course serves a number of purposes. It provides students with skills in the use of accounting systems as well as a very good overview of business operations. The accounting topics have remained rather stable over a number of years. These include the usual steps involved in the accounting cycle, accounting for the sole proprietor, accounting for a partnership, corporate accounting, and cost accounting.

What has changed is the manner in which records are kept. The computer has brought many changes and a debate over how the hardware and software should be used in the accounting courses. Two schools of thought have evolved: (1) The accounting principles and concepts should be taught manually before introducing the microcomputer and (2) introduce computer applications concurrently with teaching the basic principles and concepts manually.

Creveling and Bartholome provide an interesting review of the literature on this topic and the results of a survey of Utah accounting teachers.[18] They found: (1) nearly three-fourths of the teachers do not use computers to teach accounting; (2) one-third of the teachers who use the computer in accounting teach a separate computerized accounting course, two-thirds integrate computers into their existing courses; (3) approximately 42 percent introduce

---

[17]"State Board of Education Rules for Curriculum." Austin: Texas Education Agency, 1988.

[18]Creveling, Jan Borgmeier, and Bartholome, Lloyd W. "Integrating Computers into High School Accounting Instruction." *The Balance Sheet* 70:5; May-June 1989.

computerized accounting in the first-year course, but place more emphasis on such during the second-year course.

As one peruses the literature it seems clear the issue of *whether to use computers* in accounting is somewhat restricted to secondary schools. Community colleges and universities, usually with more financial support, have utilized computers in accounting for a number of years. However, the literature on postsecondary accounting indicates educators at this level continue to search for *the best ways* to use computers in accounting classes. For example, Selby describes how Elgin Community College uses special topics courses as the medium to allow for microcomputer instruction.[19] At her school students, upon completion of the first-semester financial accounting course, can take "Microcomputer Applications for Financial Accounting— Lotus 1-2-3," "Microcomputer Applications for Financial Accounting— General Ledger," or other special computerized topics courses in cost, intermediate, payroll, and tax accounting.

Certainly the use of computers in accounting remains an issue; that is, there are no clear cut answers about what should be done. Surely the background of the accounting instructor will have a major effect on the use of computers. As teacher education majors complete their college programs where computer coursework is required, it is expected we will see a transfer of their computer competencies to the accounting classrooms. Also, some states, such as Texas, are writing computerized accounting requirements into the state curriculum. This will force school districts to make computers available for the accounting teacher and students.

One point should not go unnoticed. If business educators will survey their communities, they will probably find considerable business use of micro-computers with accompanying accounting or financial management software. Our courses should reflect the environment in which the schools exist.

COMPUTER COURSEWORK IN BUSINESS EDUCATION

The integration of computers in each of the major business foundation subject matter areas has been discussed. Business departments also offer computer courses which are quite varied from one state to another. For this discussion, the authors choose to reference Holder's article, "Computer Competencies for Business Education Students." In the article, Holder provides a matrix of computer competencies needed by students K-12. She believes the task of providing for these competencies does not fall within the purview of a single school department or grade level. "Rather, educators from all academic disciplines must cooperate to develop a complete computer competency plan for grades K-12."[20] Business educators should be prepared to deliver some of those competencies.

The matrix addresses 10 computer competency areas: applications; pro-gramming; computer hardware, software, and systems; microcomputer

---

[19]Selby, Grace Jean. "Integrating Microcomputer Applications in Accounting." *Business Education Forum* 43:17; May 1989.

[20]Holder, Birdie H. "Computer Competencies for Business Education Students." *The Balance Sheet* 69:27; March-April 1988.

operations; computer languages; computer usages and applications in various fields; computer vocabulary (terminology); career opportunities in data processing; the effects of computers on society; and the evolution of computers.[21] Further, the matrix indicates the level—awareness, operational, or competence—that should be expected of students at the various grade levels K-12. The article provides an excellent overview of what our schools should be addressing in the computer arena. Because the matrix has been derived from research studies, it contains information on which one can justifiably base computer offerings in the business education curriculum.

As the use of computers becomes more common on a personal and professional basis, schools are going to be held accountable for turning out computer literate students. Policy Statement No. 34, "This We Believe About Computer Literacy," addresses this concern. According to the Statement, a computer literate person should be able to:

Understand the computer's capabilities and limitations

Demonstrate a fundamental knowledge of computers and their effects on society

Communicate with others using computer vocabulary

Operate the computer effectively

Access information in the computer

Input information with speed and accuracy using keyboarding skills

Use the computer as a tool for solving problems.[22]

Considering the preceding, it is likely that business education departments should deliver computer courses in literacy, applications, and programming. These would be in addition to the extensive integration of computers that is discussed previously. Certainly business educators should assume a major leadership role in computer education at the high school and postsecondary levels.

SUMMARY

This chapter has provided an overview of current thought regarding the development of basic business competencies. Business education departments should be certain that course offerings cover the general subject matter areas of concern here. Those are: economic education and personal business; business organization and management; entrepreneurship; recordkeeping and accounting; and computer science. The coursework in these areas provides students with personal and business competencies that may become survival skills for them in the future.

---

[21]*Ibid.*, pp. 29-30.

[22]"This We Believe About Computer Literacy." Policy Statement No. 34. Reston, VA: Policies Commission for Business and Economic Education, 1984.

CHAPTER 7

Business Curriculum Models from Professional Organizations

W. CLARK FORD

Middle Tennessee State University, Murfreesboro

C. STEVEN HUNT

Western Kentucky University, Bowling Green

ROY W. HEDRICK

Stephen F. Austin State University, Nacogdoches, Texas

The school curriculum is like a glacier—massive, rough and craggy on the surface; slow-moving, constantly changing; and with parts often disappearing. Glaciers are uncontrollable. Educational curriculums often appear to be the same.

In the narrow sense, a curriculum is that series of courses a person must take when enrolled in a school program in order to receive a particular diploma or major. However, learning does not take place within the walls of the classroom or the school alone. Nor is learning influenced just by the teachers and administrators within the institution.

ATMOSPHERE FOR CHANGE

A new program is like an infant. It must be nourished, cuddled, stroked, and directed as it matures. However, age, independence, and self-reliance may lead to rigidity. A rigid atmosphere can foster several problems: creativity is stifled, the willingness to experiment and try something new is lost; and the capacity to meet the challenges of a changing society is diminished.

With the increased tempo in the creation of knowledge and the development of technology, programs must be sensitive to the demands of the community. As educators in the business disciplines, our credibility is at stake. It is our responsibility to stay "in tune" with these changes and modify the curriculum to include these developments.

DEVELOPMENT OF SPECIALIZED CONTENT AREAS

With the increases in technical information comes the need for specialization. A colleague recently made this statement, "Years ago when I majored in business education, I was certified to teach everything—general business, typewriting, and bookkeeping." Even though the statement was made facetiously, it has some merit. Today's knowledge explosion has led to specialization in teacher certification and professional organizational development. Therefore, it was only natural for many organizations to develop guidelines for education programs.

The information presented in this chapter will focus on curriculum models developed for or closely related to business education. The data is from select interest groups and should not be considered all-inclusive. If the reader desires additional information, the addresses for the organizations are presented at the end of the chapter.

ASSOCIATION FOR INFORMATION SYSTEMS PROFESSIONALS (AISP)[1]

In response to the expressed needs of business and industry, the Information Systems Curriculum for Postsecondary Institutions was developed in co-operation with the Association for Information Systems Professionals. This model curriculum was designed to prepare entry-level employees to be able to understand and operate the information-based technology of today's business environment.

The scope of this model curriculum is to provide training in an open-entry/open-exit format for the high school graduate, the person desiring to update skills, and the person wanting retraining for a new career. With this in mind, the most appropriate location for the implementation of this curriculum is the one- and two-year postsecondary institutions. The model curriculum was developed with the intent of meeting the needs of students with a wide range of backgrounds to enable them to function effectively in the changing information age. A second intent included meeting the needs of business and industry by providing competent entry-level personnel, personnel who can sit for and pass a significant portion of the Certified Systems Professional (CSP) exam.

Although this curriculum can be used exclusively at the one- and two-year postsecondary institutions, it is designed so that articulation can occur between this level of education and both secondary and four-year colleges and universities. The curriculum is designed to build upon the secondary-developed skills of English grammar, keyboarding, word processing, and computer literacy. At the collegiate level the curriculum provides the basis for programs in systems management, information management, systems design, and systems analysis. These are the core courses of the Information Systems Curriculum:

1. Computer Business Applications I (reinforce and enlarge existing skills in working with integrated software)

2. Computer Business Applications II (build skills in comparing, evaluating, selecting, and manipulating software and hardware)

3. Database Systems

---

[1]O'Neil, Sharon Lund, and Everett, Donna R. *Information Systems Curriculum.* Houston: College of Technology, University of Houston, 1988.

4. Telecommunications/Networking
5. Applied Information Systems
6. Integrated Information Systems
7. Information Systems Administration (capstone course)
8. Communication for the Automated Office
9. Human Behavior in Organizations

The core courses, which have been developed into actual teaching materials, can be completed with the following subjects in completing a degree program: principles of management, records management and/or forms management, principles of accounting/managerial accounting, programming languages, entrepreneurship, economics, human relations, and similar subjects.

These competencies provide the foundation for programs or entry into several career paths including: administrative assistant, administrative services coordinator, data/word processing coordinator, information center director, information processing supervisor, information systems trainer/coordinator, office services manager, office systems specialist, and systems analyst. Because the AISP Information Systems Curriculum meshes with and can be used with several other curriculum models/materials, it offers flexibility to its users.

ASSOCIATION OF RECORDS MANAGERS AND ADMINISTRATORS, INC. (ARMA)

The Education Committee of ARMA International has developed both a two-year and a bachelor's degree program to meet the demands of the evolving records and information management profession. The purpose of the model curriculum is "to define and develop knowledge, skills, and attitudes needed by records management professionals." The curriculum is based on the current needs of both students and employers. Further, it provides necessary knowledge and skills needed in today's changing business environment. The two-year degree program will equip students with technical skills for entry-level positions such as records and information technician with possible career paths into supervisory or middle-management positions such as records and information supervisor or records center supervisor.[2]

The bachelor's degree program provides students with formal education necessary for professional advancement and promotability in office administration. With this degree, students may find entry-level positions as records and information systems analyst with possible advancement to senior positions such as records and information administrator.[3] Core courses in the two- and four-year programs are:

Two-Year	Four-Year
Principles of Records/Information Management	Introduction to Records/Information Management

[2]Association of Records Managers and Administrators (ARMA) Education Committee. *Two-Year Degree/Diploma Model Program for Records/Information Management*. Prairie Village, KS: the Association, 1988. pp. 1-3.

[3]Association of Records Managers and Administrators (ARMA) Education Committee. *Bachelor's Degree Model Program for Records/Information Management*. Prairie Village, KS: the Association, 1988. pp. 3-5.

Micrographics/Image Management
Forms Management
Archives Management
Internship

Systems and Functions of
  Records/Information Management
Specialized Functions of
  Records/Information Management
Topics for Records/Information
  Management
Cooperative Work Experience

DATA PROCESSING MANAGEMENT ASSOCIATION (DPMA)

Since the first commercially produced computer, the ENIAC, was put into operation in the 1950's, the content needed to prepare persons for computer-related careers has been debated. Throughout the last 30 years, many changes have occurred in the computer industry. As a result of the birth of the information revolution, the need to research, discuss, and insist on relevance in the teaching of data processing has become a topic of much controversy.

The unique situation of data processing education, especially at the collegiate level, has been that major programs in data processing are found in departments of mathematics, departments of computer science, colleges of engineering, or colleges of business. There seems to be a broad difference in the products when comparing graduates from these various areas of the college campus. Chances are great that the graduate has no business-oriented application experience unless it is gained from the college of business.

As early as 1979, DPMA became concerned enough about data processing education with business applications to develop a model curriculum. Each educational institution has traditionally developed data processing programs with very little uniformity with existing programs at other institutions. The DPMA model curriculum attempts to provide uniformity among programs offered at various colleges and universities. The primary objective of the DPMA Model Curriculum for Computer Information Systems is to provide graduates with the knowledge, abilities, and attitudes to function effectively as applications programmer/analysts, and with the educational background and desire for lifelong professional development.[4]

The Computer Information Systems (CIS) program was designed to be a major concentration for students in schools of business resembling the concentrations of accounting and management. Seven courses were developed as the core requirements. These seven courses include the essential concepts that all information systems personnel need.

1. Introduction to Computer-Based Systems
2. Applications Program Development I (introduction to computer programming)
3. Applications Program Development II (continuation of previous course)
4. Systems Analysis Methods
5. Structured Systems Analysis Design
6. Database Program Development
7. Applied Software Development Project

---

[4]Adams, David R., and Athey, Thomas H., editors. *DPMA Model Curriculum for Undergraduate Computer Information Systems Education.* Park Ridge, IL: Data Processing Management Association, 1981.

Of these seven courses, four are recommended for lower division and three for upper division. This allows junior colleges to interface with senior colleges and universities in the CIS program. To complete a balanced major, schools may choose three electives from the eight additional courses included in the model curriculum: Software and Hardware Concepts, Office Automation, Decision Support Systems, Advanced Database Concepts, Distributed Data Processing, EDP Audit and Controls, Information Systems Planning, and Information Resource Management. Each course is designed to be taught as a three-unit, semester-long course for a total of 30 hours.

The remainder of the course work for a baccalaureate degree consists of supporting business subjects and courses in the arts, sciences, and humanities. The list of supporting business subjects that are recommended by the model curriculum follow the pattern of AACSB core courses.

NATIONAL BUSINESS EDUCATION ASSOCIATION DATABASE OF COMPETENCIES FOR K-14[5]

The NBEA Database of Competencies for K-14 is a list of proficiency standards for entry-level employment. Developed by educators and individuals in business and industry, the competencies are based on skills, abilities, and attitudes considered essential for success in the business office.

Each of the competencies is composed of three basic parts similar to performance objectives. The first part of the competency is the condition under which the student is expected to perform. The second part is the performance or the statement of what the student is expected to do. The third part of the competency is the suggested standard, the minimum level of proficiency to be accepted.

The competencies within the database are classified according to three levels of education: elementary school, middle/junior high school, and secondary and postsecondary. The standards set for elementary and middle/junior high schools include keyboarding, basic economics, computer literacy, career and business exploration, and job attitude and human relations skills. For the secondary and postsecondary category, the standards are comprised of basic skills and core competencies, processing text skills and competencies, processing data skills (accounting and record keeping), and entrepreneurship competencies.

NBEA BUSINESS TEACHER EDUCATION CURRICULUM GUIDE[6]

Several factors have occurred in the past ten years that have brought about the need for the development of this curriculum guide. The economic recession which forced educational cutbacks, the information revolution in the United States (as well as worldwide), and the series of critical reports of teachers and teacher education programs are but a few of these factors.

---

[5]Stocker, H. Robert. "Computer Proliferation and the Changing Curriculum." *Business Education Forum* 42: 18-19, 22; March 1988.

[6]National Business Education Association. *Business Teacher Education Curriculum Guide*. Reston, VA: the Association, 1987.

Because of these critical evaluations of education and teacher preparation programs, this guide can be used effectively as a model for developing and revising business teacher education programs. It can also be used as a model for the evaluation of the curriculum by the National Council for the Accreditation of Teacher Education as well as other accrediting bodies.

This model is markedly different from others discussed in this chapter in that this curriculum does not provide a list of suggested courses with suggested course contents. However, like the database of competencies for K-14, the model curriculum for teacher education is a set of 118 competencies which should be demonstrated by graduates of collegiate teacher education programs. These competencies are grouped according to eight identified major roles of a business educator: curriculum development, instruction, evaluation, management, guidance, interpersonal communication, student organizations, and professional development.

From the list above, it should be apparent that the majority of the content of the curriculum guide is devoted to the preparation of the business educator as a professional. However, the last chapter contains recommendations to prepare business teachers to be experts in the subject matter content. The competencies of this section have been identified by the NBEA Model Curriculum Task Force (K-14) and the American Assembly of Collegiate Schools of Business (AACSB). As with other model curriculums, the NBEA Business Teacher Education Curriculum Guide stresses the necessity of learning as a lifelong process.

NATIONAL COUNCIL FOR MARKETING EDUCATION[7]

Marketing is a diverse discipline. Education for a marketing career may be at the collegiate or prebaccalaureate level. Marketing education at the prebaccalaureate level is designed to produce competent workers for the major occupational areas within marketing. Prebaccalaureate programs also include high school level study.

The four-year college programs approach marketing education from the managerial perspective. Most of the attention is devoted to theory rather than practical, day-to-day operations. Programs at this level offer baccalaureate, master's, or higher-level degrees. Prebaccalaureate programs at the high school and community/technical college place emphasis on applied marketing—applications of specific skills and concepts for the daily operations of a business.

Rather than identify core courses a student should take, the National Council on Marketing Education has recommended a core of competency areas which must be mastered by the student in order to enter and maintain employment at various levels. The levels for which competencies are sought are entry level, career-sustaining, marketing specialist, marketing supervisor, and manager/entrepreneur.

---

[7]National Council for Marketing Education. *National Curriculum Framework and Core Competencies.* Columbus, OH: the Council, 1987.

The competency core includes a study of two broad areas: foundations of marketing and functions of marketing.

Foundations of marketing includes three broad areas in the foundations segment:

1. *Economics of marketing*—Basic economic principles and concepts of free-enterprise and free-marketing economics that are fundamental to an understanding of marketing activities.

2. *Human resources*—Basic, generic skills and understanding critical to success in many occupations, including aspects of human relations, communications, and math.

3. *Marketing and business*—Basic skills and understanding of the marketing concept, the business environment, and the management systems within which it is implemented.

The marketing segment includes distribution, financing, marketing-information management, pricing, product/service planning, promotion, purchasing, risk management, and selling. The depth of study in each of the functions will be determined by the level of competency sought by the student and teacher.

OFFICE SYSTEMS RESEARCH ASSOCIATION (OSRA)

With encouragement from business and industry to develop collegiate programs to address more specifically office systems education, OSRA accepted the challenge and sponsored the development of a Model Curriculum for Office Systems. The structure of the curriculum is presented within a framework of 10 three-semester-credit courses:

Core Courses	Optional Courses
OS1-Office Systems & Technologies	OS6-Telecommunications
OS2-Office Systems Planning	OS7-Administrative Communications
OS3-Office Systems Implementation Strategies	OS8-Training/Development in Office Systems
OS4-Office Systems Applications	OS9-Special Topics in Office Systems
OS5-Integrated Office Systems	OS10-Professional Practice in Office Systems

This framework is flexible, and course content may be included in programs in many other forms. Content may be split between/among courses or within courses with other titles and still remain consistent with the intent of the model. Educational institutions adopting the model may adapt the model to fit their needs and requirements in terms of course sequencing and prerequisites. The model is designed for four-year schools and includes general education courses, standard business courses, office systems core courses, and office systems optional courses.

The curriculum is designed to enable graduates to (a) analyze office activities, (b) plan for and design appropriate office systems, (c) implement new office technologies and (d) evaluate and manage the new office systems. Further, this curriculum emphasizes the human aspect of the office, as contrasted with existing computer science curriculums which emphasize hardware and software. Graduates will be "user-oriented" as well as prepared to plan and to manage the change effort necessary to the introduction of new technologies.[8]

The OSRA curriculum should provide the essential foundation for assuming an array of employment opportunities. Occupational specialties such as office systems analyst, office systems manager, word processing administrator, and marketing support representative—as well as career paths in educational consulting and training—exist for those pursuing the office systems major.

PROFESSIONAL SECRETARIES INTERNATIONAL (PSI)[9]

In an effort to meet the challenges of tomorrow with a responsive curriculum, PSI also has undertaken the task of sponsoring the development of a curriculum model to be used at the postsecondary level in the preparation of office professionals. The PSI curriculum was developed on the idea that the office workers to today and tomorrow need to be flexible, adaptable, and capable of accepting change if they are to contribute to the productivity of the evolving office environment.

The Postsecondary Model Curriculum for Office Professionals has been designed for adaptation in all postsecondary-level programs. Specifically, it has been designed for programs in independent colleges, junior/community colleges, vocational-technical schools, adult education, and two-year programs in colleges and universities. The model's flexible nature provides job skills at the end of any semester of study. The goal of an associate degree is supported by progressive semesters of traditional study or adult/continuous education courses.

This model is flexible in its arrangement, making it adaptable in a variety of programming situations within various types of institutions. The flexibility of the model is enhanced by well-defined entry and exit points which give recognition to previously acquired skills and knowledges upon entry and give realistic employment expectations at time of exit. The model is focused on six separate, but not dissimilar, outcomes, including: qualification to sit for entry-level certification, attainment of an associate's degree, specialization in structured career paths, specialized training, qualification to sit for CPS rating, and employment.

The specific courses within the curriculum are shown by semester.

Year One

*Semester 1	Semester 2
Document Formatting	Document Production/Word Processing
Administrative Systems and Procedures	Business Communication
Fundamentals of Communications	Advanced Word Processing Applications

---

[8]Office Systems Curriculum Group. *The Office Systems Research Association Model Curriculum for Office Systems Education.* Cincinnati: South-Western Publishing Co., 1986. pp. 1-3.

[9]Professional Secretaries International (PSI). *PSI Postsecondary Model Curriculum for Office Careers.* Kansas City, MO: PSI, 1988. pp. 1-5.

| Information Processing Concepts and Applications | Advanced Information Processing Applications |

*The first semester requires a prerequisite of keyboarding skills

The second year of study can integrate the third and fourth semesters of study to meet institutional scheduling and the student's career objectives. The suggested courses that comprise this curriculum lead to meeting the requirements for the CPS certification and specialization. During the third semester, courses in office supervision, office systems and technology, and Accounting I are recommended as well as two courses in a specialty area, e.g., desktop publishing, information processing, office systems, and legal and medical courses. Since the ultimate goal of this curriculum is to receive an associate degree and provide adequate training to sit for the CPS examination, each institution must give attention to the specific content areas of the CPS examination. Therefore, courses in the fourth semester of the curriculum should include Behavioral Science in Business/Applied Psychology, Business Law, Economics, Principles of Management, and Accounting II.

THE IMPORTANCE OF CURRICULUM MODELS

Each of the curriculum models presented here were designed to be dynamic and evolutionary in preparing students for a progressive, change-oriented business and office environment. The models generally, and the individual courses specifically, have addressed the changes in technology, skills in business and the office, and career path options. These dimensions provide the results of workable curriculum models that are responsive to the needs of today but sensitive to the trends of tomorrow.

IMPLICATIONS FOR TEACHERS IN THE BUSINESS DISCIPLINES

What is the teacher's role in the total educational process? Must the teacher be the scientist who finds the cure for the illness, the doctor who diagnoses the illness and prescribes the medicine, the pharmacist who fills the prescription, or the nurse who administers the medicine to the patient? Can you, as a teacher, be everything to everyone?

The information revolution—like the agricultural and industrial revolutions before it—will have profound and long-lasting cultural, social, and educational implications. Lifestyles, social patterns, the work environment—as well as the conduct of business—will change as new skills and technologies replace older, often well-established, ones.

Business educators, by knowing that experts are available for consultation, can move with confidence in their own program development. The teacher's burden or feeling that "I must be the creator of all, the knower of all, and the disseminator of all" is eliminated. Teachers can concentrate on determining what is most beneficial for the students in their local community, and in preparing their graduates to face reality in the educational environment as well as the corporate sector.

77

With these curriculum guidelines, business educators have an avenue for restructuring and modifying traditional program offerings. To implement such new curriculums, a mutually viable alliance among manufacturers, the business community, and academe must exist so that all parties concerned can share experiences and resources and thus become better attuned to dynamic developments in applied technology-based office operations. Rapid changes in office operations and the information age mandate that business educators assess how they might best implement a viable and relevant program for training office professionals.

If these guidelines are to gain wide acceptance at colleges and universities and if graduates of such programs are to achieve recognition for their expertise, the curriculum and concomitant components must be disseminated to the appropriate audiences. Collaboration of all those involved in the business disciplines will help achieve this goal.

Business educators cannot afford to be complacent or negligent in responding to current labor market needs. By developing appropriate academic courses not only at the high school level but also at the undergraduate and graduate levels, business education can ensure both its survival and its ability to respond to the needs of the technology-based office work force.

DIRECTORY OF ORGANIZATIONS

ASSOCIATION FOR INFORMATION
  SYSTEMS PROFESSIONALS
104 Wilmot Road, Suite 201
Deerfield, IL 60015-5195

ASSOCIATION OF RECORDS MANAGEMENT
  AND ADMINISTRATORS
4200 Somerset, Suite 215
Prairie Village, KS 66208

DATA PROCESSING MANAGEMENT
  ASSOCIATION
505 Busse Highway
Park Ridge, IL 60068

NATIONAL BUSINESS EDUCATION
  ASSOCIATION
1914 Association Drive
Reston, VA 22091

NATIONAL COUNCIL FOR MARKETING
  EDUCATION
Marketing Education Resource Center
1375 King Avenue
P.O. Box 12226
Columbus, OH 43212-0226

OFFICE SYSTEMS RESEARCH
  ASSOCIATION
501 Grise Hall
College of Business Administration
Western Kentucky University
Bowling Green, KY 42101

PROFESSIONAL SECRETARIES,
  INTERNATIONAL
310 East Armour Boulevard
Kansas City, MO 64111-1299

CHAPTER 8

Exemplary Business Education Programs in the United States

Global economy, entrepreneurship, productivity, technology, aging population, information age—these are frequently used buzz words. What do they mean to business teachers? Students are willing; industry is waiting; technology is exciting; educators are responding; meaningful new programs are resulting. This chapter presents concepts for new and innovative programs and plans that have been developed and implemented in five different states to enhance student involvement, interaction, and learning.

Section A: Technology—Program Course Approaches (Connecticut)

JOAN S. BRIGGAMAN
Connecticut State Department of Education, Middletown

By the time this Yearbook is published, what is covered in this section as "the cutting edge" of technology will be commonplace. While new models with enhanced capabilities hit the market every day, the major areas of technology that will impact business education in the foreseeable future have been identified. Our challenge is to develop programs that teach this technology.

THE QUESTION

If the challenge is to teach technology, then the question is, what constitutes the technology we should be teaching? What we teach should reflect what we find in the business world. This means we need to seek input from the business community through advisory committees, business visits, and keeping up to date through the media and work experience opportunities. A walk through any up-to-date business office today would put the items listed below on the technology list.

- *Computer systems*—mouse, hard disk, laser printers, communications capability
- *Touch-tone telephones*—to allow key responses to computer inquiries and voice messaging
- *Fax*—not a new technology, but one that has come down in cost and up in quality and versatility

- *Copiers*—with microprocessors, capable of receiving copy from computers via telephone and completing multiple functions such as collating, covering, and binding before documents leave the machine
- *Telecommunications*—through the computer and telephone lines, the ability to access thousands of data/information bases, networks, and upload and download information
- *Software*—desktop publishing, electronic mail, multifunction, simulation, authoring, report generating, and management systems.

Is this everything? No, but it reflects the major areas from which the hybrids will spring.

THE ISSUES

Now that the technology has been determined, the issues that need to be resolved become clear. Should technology be taught in special courses or integrated? Should individual learning activity packages (LAP's) be developed or whole classes taught at one time? What are the basic skills of the technology? What are the advanced skills of the technology? Which students need which skill levels? How can the instruction be developed from simple to complex? How can use of the technology be scheduled so that all students develop appropriate competency? How can teachers be taught the technology? How can the administration be encouraged to allocate the funds?

THE ANSWERS

There are no easy answers to these problems, nor will the answer be the same for each school; every business department must work out the answers. Some points, however, are not negotiable.

- Technology must be shared by all subject areas on an equitable basis. This means students and teachers will have to change and share rooms.
- Integration into existing courses rather than separate courses will be required because there are not enough students or hours to add new courses. Integration also shows students how the technology relates and enhances the subject.
- Not every student needs to know everything. In order to provide competency levels for all students, it becomes critical to identify the minimum competencies for each subject and teach those. Once all students have mastered the minimum competencies, then and only then can advanced use of the technology be taught.
- Many applications require interaction so that students, teachers, and classes need to work as teams to really master the technology.
- Mastery of technology will be different for each student. Individualized LAP's should be developed for students. They will also assist teachers to master the technology.

THE MODELS

The models discussed below are based on the premise that basic keyboarding/word processing has been taught and that students are user-friendly with computers.

Telecommunications

Equipment. Dedicated telephone lines, computers with telecommunications capabilities, compatible word processsing software.

Subject area. Office procedures, accounting.

Application. Use an office simulation as the basis to upload/download documents for processing by the receiving class.

Strengths. Students not only learn team work, they become competent in the use of the computer to telecommunicate information.

Problems. Centered around getting started and cost of maintaining and securing telephone lines.

External Databases

Equipment. Computer with telecommunications capability, software to telecommunicate, telephone lines connected to the computer.

Subject area. Economics, law, basic business, etc.

Application. Access external and CD ROM databases, such as Dow Jones, Law Journal, Books in Print, newspapers, etc., to obtain data to prepare reports, and projects, make decisions, and solve problems.

Strengths. Can be individual, team, or class assignments; teaches and reinforces a variety of skills and knowledge.

Problems. Availability of equipment and funds to access databases.

Solution. Work with the school's library/media center.

Networks

Equipment. Computer with telecommunications capability, software to telecommunicate, telephone line connected to the computer.

Application. Access various networks to leave and receive messages.

Fax

Equipment. Fax machine and telephone line.

Application. Need two stations, preferably in two different schools or towns. Use a simulation to have students send/receive and process documents. Emphasis should be on when to use fax, telephone, or mail to process documents.

Touch-Tone Telephones

Equipment. Touch-tone telephone, voice link or computer-link capability.

Application. Contact your local telephone company to determine if they are participating in a voice link project and if they will include your students. Through use of touch-tone telephone, students are able to leave voice messages for others, listen to messages left for them, save or delete messages, and respond to messages previously stored. Vendors may also be willing to participate in pilots.

Desktop Publishing

Equipment. Hard disk computer, mouse, scanner, laser printer, software.

Application. Students learn to use scanner and mouse to enhance typical documents and print single copies that will be duplicated on state-of-the-art copiers, or enhanced document can be sent via telecommunications directly to copier for duplication.

THE BOTTOM LINE

The models presented here are only teasers to whet the appetite and to provoke thinking and the realization that there is no limit to what can be created. The only barriers are those you build for yourself. With the issues and answers discussed above as a guide, we can use any new technology that comes along and impacts on the business world to help our students get the best jobs.

Section B: An International Business Program (Ohio)

CHARLOTTE COOMER

Ohio State Department of Education, Columbus

Students are different today: they respond differently to the business curriculum and demonstrate different values from students a decade ago. Business educators continue to search for unique strategies to reach students. Only one conclusion can be reached—the world is changing. The degree to which business educators have accepted the challenges of world change determines, in part, the success of their abilities to teach today's students.

Many school districts in Ohio have responded positively to these changes. Numerous Japanese-based companies have located in Ohio communities, in addition to other new businesses with parent-based companies in Spain, Great Britain, or other countries. After 18 months of careful planning, a vocational program for international business managers was implemented for high school juniors and seniors in one of Ohio's cities. The planning included interviews with corporate executives, monthly meetings of the very specialized advisory committee, curriculum planning and development, student and teacher recruitment, and program promotion.

The operational procedures of the program include weekly visits to sponsoring businesses. Each of the students in the program is sponsored by a management-level employee in the international division of the corporation or a community leader involved in international practices. Another novel but necessary component of the program is the link with foreign languages. Each of the students enrolled has either completed at least one year of a foreign language or is enrolled simultaneously in such a class. Although the foreign language class is not currently included in the formal program structure and curriculum document, the communications component addresses the integration of foreign languages. The students spend three hours each day in the program.

To be successful, the students must first be interested in the curriculum and must express career interests associated with international business. Whether parents, citizens, and educators agree with the present state of the world economy and its accompanying trade practices is not the issue. Each student must have identified employment in the field of international business as an immediate or long-range career objective. More specific career objectives within the realm of international business are expected to emerge for each student throughout the span of the two-year curriculum.

In a global society with trade restrictions and policies that affect business on a daily basis, the goal of the students in the international business manager program is to demonstrate the most effective methods of conducting business in a society linked through goods and services, technology, and inter-dependence. Unlike the generic concept of global education, the international business manager program focuses on a specific curriculum with duties and tasks designed to assist the students in functioning in business, either immediately after high school or after completing additional business studies —often in conjunction with a four-year international business program in college. The following duties—with specific objectives, student performance activities, and instructional strategies—are part of the program:

1. Utilize a computer terminal.
2. Keyboard Information.
3. Apply economic principles.
4. Conduct world trade.
5. Manage resources.
6. Create a new business.
7. Apply business law.
8. Perform accounting functions.
9. Work in an office environment.
10. Communicate with others.
11. Perform business procedures.
12. Secure employment.
13. Develop and practice proper business safety.
14. Participate in a vocational student organization.

As indicated, each student spends approximately three hours each week with the personnel in the sponsoring businesses. Sponsors also volunteer time to visit the class and contribute time and expertise to the entire group. For example, those students who are preparing to enter competitive events in the Business Professionals of America program are provided specific expertise.

All facets of the student's educational program are integrated in the inter-national business manager curriculum. Math, communications, world geography, application of technology, and personal development are all important components of the curriculum.

This program is but one example of the educational opportunities that can be extended to students when the dynamic energies of business communities and educators are combined. The implications of the concepts of this program are crucial for all business programs, regardless of the specific involvement of the community in terms of international trade. All business programs should include concepts that assist students in understanding the importance of applying the appropriate business etiquette, communications, and human relations to be successful in our society—a society that includes people from many countries and cultures. Because technology has linked the people of the world, business educators must assist students in meeting the challenges of conducting business beyond the local community, the home state, and the United States. Business educators must continue to be alert to the needs of local businesses to equip students with the skills, knowledge, and attitudes needed to function in a multicultural, complex business environment.

Section C: Quality—A Continuous Improvement Process (Arizona)

JANET M. GANDY
Arizona State Department of Education, Phoenix

In the modern world of global competition and rising customer expectations of higher quality, lower cost, and faster product development, both private and public organizations feel mounting pressure to improve the quality of their products and service. It is estimated that one-fourth of all work in America is done to find and correct errors.[1] Significantly reducing that fraction would allow organizations to increase their productivity without increasing their costs. Rather than adding to costs, improving quality lowers them—mainly because it holds down or eliminates costs of finding and fixing mistakes. Can you imagine the sense of satisfaction we would all have about our work if everyone at every level were actively involved in the quality improvement process—accountable for everything they did and striving for continuous improvement?

America's commercial and defense industries are working toward an integrated system of industrial and management processes applying continuous improvement resulting in Total Quality Management (TQM). Acceptance of this system in America is driven by the need to compete. With TQM, cost and time to produce a product can be cut in half. Overall quality, as defined by the customer, is improved manyfold. Hewlett Packard has been under way with its total quality management system for 10 years. Boeing, Ford Motor Company, Xerox, IBM, ITT and Kodak are examples of other companies which are well into TQM programs.

For over 40 years the Japanese have been developing total quality management for their commercial industries with the help of W. Edwards Deming,

---

[1] "Training for Quality." *INFO-LINE*, May 1988. p. 1.

Joseph Juran, Genichi Taguchi, and others. An advanced industrial/management system has evolved which is creating a second industrial revolution. Dr. Deming's approach to TQM is based on the functioning of a detailed and interlocked system. His system starts and ends with the customer, both internal and external. Through the use of statistical techniques, higher quality will be achieved at lower cost. Dr. Deming's methods involve long-range commitment, attention to customers, hands-on leadership, teamwork, continual improvement in all processes, individual achievement, innovative design, attention to detail, and shared rewards. The fundamental principle to his system is "do it right the first time." Navy officials say that through application of the "do it right the first time" principle, a 52-week backlog at their Naval Aviation Depot in California has been slashed to two weeks and better quality has resulted.[2]

The fundamental maxim of Dr. Taguchi's theory is to assure the consistent quality of a product; it must have quality designed into every step of the process. Building quality in at each step actually cuts cost, as evidenced at a division of ITT. After adopting Taguchi's techniques, the company reported their defects in products were cut in half saving some $60 million between 1985 and 1987.[3]

Lest the benefits of TQM seem too good to be true, consider that it is a difficult process for a company to embrace. It involves active commitment to creating a comprehensive cultural change from the top of the organization down. Achieving lasting quality improvement will require fundamental changes in the way organizations are run, including changes in values and philosophies of business, refocused roles of management and supervision, modified incentive systems, and training everyone in statistical thinking techniques to enable workers to speak a common language and contribute to the decision-making process.

As more industries adopt the TQM philosophy and recognize there is no short cut to long-term improvement—only commitment to setting and meeting higher standards—there will be an increase in the need for in-depth training. Training is the foundation on which successful quality improvement is built.

Perhaps through training students in total quality management, the educational system itself will undergo a cultural revolution in its business of educating. Public education can be a primary delivery for training everyone in the continuous improvement process. A commitment by our educational system to teaching today's students—tomorrow's workers—this process will benefit all American industries and the country as a whole to increase U.S. competitiveness.

To determine if the continuous improvement process could effectively be transferred from the industrial setting to a classroom, the Vocational Division of the Arizona Department of Education facilitated a pilot partnership between a company practicing the process, McDonnell Douglas Helicopter,

[2] "The Deming Way's New Battleground: The Defense Dept." *The Washington Post.* May 29, 1988.

[3] Chapple, Alan. "Engineers Look to Quality Techniques To Fend Off Foreign Challenge." *Engineering Times.* September 1987.

and Gilbert High School. Two business teachers joined McDonnell Douglas employees receiving training in the process. The team—the teachers and the trainer—applied the process to the classroom activities at Gilbert High School in such areas as: what was taught, methods used in teaching, and the use of technology in instruction. It was determined that areas of waste were evident, and with further study, viable solutions for improvement and higher quality could be recommended.

One year later the team was expanded to include a computer-instructor from Mt. Edgecumbe High School in Sitka, Alaska. Together they developed a curriculum to support a new course called "Work" (not an acronym). Twenty-eight freshmen enrolled in this elective course at Gilbert High School to learn to use diagnostic and statistical tools, apply problem-solving processes to eliminate waste and improve the quality of their own work while using critical thinking to make decisions about projects studied as a team or individual. The curriculum of "Work" also is taught through four levels of computer education at Mt. Edgecumbe High School.

As a result of this process, teachers now facilitate the student's learning, and students take responsibility for their own learning. The difference in commitment to learning is remarkable when everyone practices total quality management of their work.

According to industry executives who have adopted the TQM philosophy and are retraining their workers in continuous improvement, the Gilbert High School and Mt. Edgecumbe High School students are gaining that competitive edge in the labor market. Imagine how quickly America's industries could regain their position in world markets if there were a national movement in public education toward total quality management.

Section D: An Approach to Entrepreneurship Training (Arkansas)

TOMMIE BUTLER
Arkansas State Department of Education, Little Rock

Searching for new curriculum designs, exciting teaching techniques, and innovative subject materials is a continuous process for business educators. Most of these educators enthusiastically accept the challenge of training their students for a successful career as an office employee. Business educators are very comfortable teaching regular office skills and a large percentage of them have updated their teaching skills in the new office technology. Many exciting computer technology training programs are now being provided for business students throughout the United States. The changes that have taken place in business education classrooms have been phenomenal.

In the last few decades both the business community and educators became concerned about surveys and research reports that indicated a general lack of understanding and appreciation for the American free enterprise system by young people. For this great system to prosper and grow, it became evident that its people must be better informed about its components, merits, and demerits. According to Clayton and Johnson's chapter entitled "Business Administration and Entrepreneurship" in the 1981 NBEA Yearbook, each decade seems to bring additional movement toward developing economic literacy. They state:

> With the advent of the *economic education movement* especially during the sixties and the *free enterprise movement* during the seventies, interest has been further kindled in business administration and entrepreneurship for the secondary school student. Because of business administration's and entrepreneurship's close relationship to these movements and a large amount of governmental funding in the late seventies to incorporate business ownership and management concepts into the curriculum at various levels of education, the eighties may foster the *entrepreneurship movement* with a new surge toward small business ownership education.[1]

It is evident that small businesses play a vital role in the American economy. The White House Commission on Small Business reported that over 80 percent of the nation's new jobs have been generated by new and existing companies in recent years. What kind of educational programs are needed to train young entrepreneurs to own and operate successful business ventures?

A STATE'S RESPONSE

Arkansas business educators have responded to the new exciting movement toward entrepreneurship training. In 1974 a proposal was funded to study the skills and knowledge necessary for this type of educational program. In developing an entrepreneurial course content guide for Arkansas high school students, over two hundred business people were surveyed and asked to study a list of entrepreneurial skills, and to indicate which ones they considered most important. A committee of business teachers studied the results carefully and selected the following units of study: leadership development, human relations, microcomputers, data processing, business ownership principles, financial management, personnel management, business communications, taxes and governmental regulations, marketing and advertising, business law, protecting assets, personal finance, and career opportunities.

The correct title for a successful course is always crucial, it would have to attract both young men and women as participants. "Junior Executive Training" seemed to be an appropriate title. The students themselves shortened the title to JET; in fact, in some schools they became known as the "JET set." The competencies expected by the participants are geared toward average and above-average students in the eleventh and twelfth grades.

EXECUTIVE BUSINESS GAME

The executive business game has become an exciting component of the Junior Executive Training program. This game is a cooperative effort between

[1]Clayton, Dean and Johnson, Phyllis J. "Business Administration and Entrepreneurship." *Updating Content in Secondary Business Education.* Nineteenth Yearbook. Reston, VA: National Business Education Association, 1981. Chapter 5, p. 54.

a state utility company, Arkansas Power & Light Company, and the Vocational Division of the Department of Education, ably assisted by personnel on the campuses of four Arkansas universities.

Teams are developed on local high school campuses, usually in a business education classroom. Officers are elected to manage the production company. These teams are in competition with eight or nine other local school teams which comprise one "industry." Since the development of the first game, the program has experienced tremendous growth, from six pilot teams in 1972 to eighty teams in 1989.

The excitement generated by this game is unbelievable. In playing the game, the team functions in three fundamental areas of management: marketing, production, and finance. Students gain valuable experience and insight into the economic realities faced by management in performing these functions as well as an appreciation of management principles and how they are universal in their application. Much of the emphasis is on planning and decision making.

Through the game, participants are put in charge of every aspect of a production business for eight simulated quarters. They are responsible for all of the decision making from inventory control to research and development. Each week their decisions are fed into computers on cooperating university campuses. Results are returned to the classroom where students review their progress and alter them accordingly. The goal, as in boardrooms across the country, is a good rate of return to stockholders and beating out the competition.

The areas in which decisions are made each week (which simulates a three-month period in the life of a real business) include: (1) product price, (2) marketing budget allocation, (3) research/development budget, (4) maintenance expenses, (5) number of units for production, (6) new investment in plant and equipment, (7) raw material purchases, and (8) amount of money (if any) to be declared as a dividend.

As in a business, students learn they have to communicate effectively; through biennial written reports to the stockholders and oral presentations at simulated annual meetings they sharpen their skills. Regional winners in all three categories compete at the state level and a trophy is awarded at the FBLA state conference each year.

Each team is judged in three areas: rate of return to the stockholders, written business report, and oral presentation to the stockholders (three judges from business, industry, and education). In addition to learning that profit is necessary to stay in business, the students are given the opportunity to develop civic awareness. During the oral presentation, the judges question the officers of the company intensively about the company's involvement in community affairs.

IMPLEMENTING THE PROGRAM

Training booklets have been developed by Arkansas Power & Light Company and distributed to each company officer on local teams. A one-day training program is held on the campuses of the four participating universities. Teachers are allowed to bring several students each to the training program each year.

It is sometimes difficult to persuade business teachers to participate in the game. Many of them have not had enough training, education, or experience to understand how corporations operate. Therefore, they do not know how to train their students to make logical business decisions of this magnitude. In addition, there is a tremendous amount of time and effort involved in the game play. Since many teachers feel overloaded, they are not receptive to taking on additional responsibilities. Those who take the risk and watch their students mature and grow in the area of entrepreneurship training agree that the executive business game is a tremendous experience for both them and their students.

Of equal importance is the cooperation of the teacher educators on the university campuses. They are responsible for accepting the decisions during the eight weeks of game play, managing the computer manipulations, mailing the computer printouts to each local team weekly, preparing for the oral presentations, and providing judges for the events. Four district competitions are held, and a state play-off is developed to determine the overall state winners.

Officials at Arkansas Power & Light Company play a vital role as a support system. Not only do they print and distribute the training booklets, but they also act as judges and consultants, provide meals for the teachers and students at the district and state competition, and furnish certificates to the winning teams.

State Department of Education personnel persuade teachers to form teams, organize the teams into industries, plan and implement the training programs, and provide teacher travel funds for the state play-off. In general, they support and encourage the total program in every possible manner. While a great deal of responsibility, time, and effort are expended to make the Junior Executive Training program and the executive business game successful, everyone involved seems to agree that these activities are worthwhile and should be continued.

Section E: Providing for Adult Learners (Oklahoma)

BETTY C. FRY

Central State University, Edmond, Oklahoma

The United States is rapidly becoming a nation of adults. Current demographic trends reveal that the median age of the population is just over 30; approximately 50 percent of all females are in the labor force; and Americans are living and, in many cases, working longer. In addition to working longer, individuals are changing careers or beginning careers later in life. Factors contributing to these changes are the emphasis on information, the impact of the computer, and changing career and life patterns of the dislocated worker and the displaced homemaker.

With this information in mind, the area vocational technical schools in Oklahoma explored ways to accommodate the increasing training needs of adults returning to work or desiring to upgrade skills for the purpose of moving within the labor force. Classrooms were equipped with the latest technology and educational materials. Although secondary students were given priority placement in the business and office programs, adults who needed training were allotted positions in existing programs. The practice of "slotting in" adults in the existing programs met both the needs of the students, program planners, and facilitators and the needs of business and industry. Adults could enter the programs at specified times and exit upon achievement of determined competency levels. This open-entry, open-exit concept has been in place for some time and continues to be appropriate for our changing educational needs.

WHAT QUESTIONS MUST THE PLANNERS AND EDUCATORS CONSIDER?

Questions such as, "Will the adults and high school students function as well in the same classroom?" and "How will the teacher make the program work with the different age groups together?" were asked frequently at the outset of the program. Educators who administer and who direct these programs feel their decisions to give it a try were good ones because the concept has worked effectively where planning and forethought have guided the implementation of effective programs.

Considerations for adult/secondary open-entry, open-exit programs include the following:

1. Does the teacher accept the concept of side-by-side training for adults and high school students?

2. Has the teacher been exposed to methodology in teaching the multi-age groups?

3. Is sufficent time provided for the teacher and staff to develop individualized instructional materials to accommodate the open-entry, open-exit concept which so often better meets the needs of the adults?

4. Is the teacher prepared for the adult who remains in the classroom for a full day (six hours) as opposed to the high school student who comes for one-half day (three hours) either in the morning or in the afternoon?

5. Because student organizations are an integral part of the programs, are teachers prepared to provide opportunities for involvement for both secondary and adult students?

There must be positive answers to the questions in order for administrators and teachers to develop programs to meet the needs of the adults and secondary students.

HOW DOES THE PROGRAM WORK?

Depending upon variables such as the number of business faculty, the entry times for adults, input from the advisory committees, and the philosophy of the school, the following scenario describes a typical program.

1. The student seeks information from the school about training programs in the various fields of business. Sometimes the student needs counseling concerning fields of interest.

2. The student is directed to the counselor or director of the program of interest and is interviewed for the purpose of determining how and where to begin.

3. Some placement tests may be given to assist in determining the background of knowledge and the proper direction for the student.

4. The interview combined with the assessment tests provide the counselor or director with information to channel the student into a program of interest.

5. If the program is developed in the cluster approach, core competencies have been identified and provide the starting point for the student in the business cluster. The cluster may identify such areas of emphasis as secretarial, micro-computer applications, and accounting.

6. If the student needs help with the basic skill areas such as language arts and mathematics, the learning resource center can be of assistance. This center serves the entire school by working with students referred with identified areas of need. The program teacher can then devote classroom time to the specific study areas for the business cluster.

7. Students may begin regardless of the time they enter the program because the instructional materials are geared to individual achievement of identified competencies. Students should not feel abandoned to a machine or book. One teacher of a program of this type recently said that she worked with each student personally during each half-day block. If students remained enrolled in the program for the full day, they consulted at least twice during each half-day block. Students with specific problems receive immediate assistance.

8. Group instruction complements the self-paced activities where appropriate. Teacher/student involvement and interaction are key to the effectiveness of the instruction. Interaction between students is achieved through group activities emphasizing communication skills, job interview techniques, and student organization activities. The development of leadership skills is extremely important to adult as well as secondary students. Guest speakers and field trips enhance bridging the gap between theory and reality.

WILL THIS PROGRAM CONCEPT MEET STUDENT NEEDS?

With the needs in the information age labor force and the needs of the adult influenced by changing life patterns and careers, instructional programs must be responsive to meeting new demands. The concept described in this section can provide an effective alternative where adult students are involved and the programs are successful.

Business educators must continue to be on the cutting edge preparing students for the changing world through innovative and challenging instructional programs. The concepts and approaches presented in this chapter represent a glimpse of meaningful programs which address the global economy, entrepreneurship, productivity, technology, information age, and the aging population.

CHAPTER 9

Reaching High Risk Populations Through Business Education

DONNA HOLMQUIST
University of Nebraska at Omaha, Omaha

BIRDIE H. HOLDER
University of Nebraska-Lincoln, Lincoln

DAVID E. GRAY
University of Missouri-Columbia, Columbia

As one reviews the demographics of our society, it becomes abundantly clear that we can no longer afford the luxury of providing education and job training for only those who actively seek it. The population is shifting from a youthful one to an elderly one, and this shift will continue into the next century. Within the next 30 years those people 65 and older will comprise almost 25 percent of our total population. At the same time that the population is aging, the birthrate is declining. The change in the age of the population and the smaller pool of young people will cause a major decline in the workforce.

As the number in the work force is going down, the number of specialized jobs is on the increase. Of the top 10 jobs for the 1990's, business education training will be required by four—secretaries, office clerks, salespeople, and retail workers.

With this demographic information available, business educators can no longer teach only those who seek the business curriculum. Business education teachers must actively recruit special populations to train for business education careers. Strategies must be developed which help to retain and educate high-risk populations so that there will be a well-trained work force for the next decade.

CHARACTERISTICS OF HIGH-RISK POPULATIONS

Three types of high-risk populations are identified in this article: handicapped, disadvantaged, and a special youth-at-risk category.

Handicapped. Handicapped populations include the following: (a) the learning disabled—individuals who are characterized by problems in the basic pyschological processes or problems in language which cause a severe discrepancy between ability and academic achievement; (b) the mentally retarded—individuals who are characterized by significantly subaverage intellectual functioning with deficits in adaptive behavior; (c) the behaviorally disordered—those whose behavior deviates from that of their peer group to the extent that it interferes with their own growth or that of others; (d) the physically handicapped—students who have orthopedic or health impairments which adversely affect their educational performance; (e) the hearing impaired—deaf and hard-of-hearing people whose educational performance is adversely affected by the hearing defect; (f) the vision impaired—a group that includes the blind, the partially sighted, and the visually limited; and (g) the speech impaired—a handicap that draws unfavorable attention to the speaker, interferes with communication, or causes the speaker to be socially maladjusted.[1]

Disadvantaged. Jerry L. Wircenski describes the disadvantaged individual as one who is "culturally, socially, educationally, and economically deprived." He further describes the disadvantaged learners as those who are reading below grade level, who have slow to retarded math ability, and who are apathetic toward school.[2]

While faculty and administrators tend to discuss the disadvantaged student in terms of ability to grasp information, a description of the environmental elements rather than personal characteristics is more apt to be used to identify the disadvantaged person. Gary Meers, in *Handbook of Vocational Special Needs Education*, identified these environmental elements as: family income at or below national poverty level; parent, guardian, and/or individual is unemployed; parent, guardian, and/or individual is recipient of public assistance; irregular school attendance; poor grades; and conflicts with teachers and/or police.[3]

High-risk. Another group of special needs individuals which has been identified as high-risk are "young people between the ages of 14 and 19 who are functionally illiterate and lack any skills for employment. . . . Within this population [is identified] individuals with special needs: pregnant teenagers, non-English-speaking aliens, in-school underachievers, and high school dropouts."[4]

As educators are planning strategies for the at-risk student, they should remember that "low socioeconomic status coupled with minority group status are strong predictors of dropping out" of school.[5]

LEGISLATION FOR THE HIGH-RISK STUDENT

Within these high-risk populations of the handicapped, the disadvantaged, or the youth-at-risk are many who can become productive workers in the

---

[1]Jacobs, Brian C. "Methods of Mainstreaming in Business and Marketing Education." *Journal of Business Education* 58:52-56; November 1982.

[2]Meers, Gary, editor. *Handbook of Vocational Special Needs Education.* (Revised edition). Rockville, MD: Aspen Publishers, 1987. pp. 47-49.

[3]*Ibid.*, pp. 7-9.

[4]Huntington Association. "Youth at Risk and Work: New York's Investment in the Future." Working paper for the Committee for Public/Private Cooperation for an Institute, 1982.

[5]Wehlage, Gary G.; Rutter, Robert A.; and Turnbaugh, Anne. "A Program Model for At-risk High School Students." *Educational Leadership* 44:70-73; March 1987.

business world. These high-risk populations and their ability to contribute have been recognized over the years by special legislation at the federal level.

As far back as the Civil War, rehabilitation legislation has been debated by the United States Congress. However, because the Constitution leaves the education of its citizens to the states, there has been a reluctance to pass laws that would usurp states' rights. But over the last three decades, there have been several laws passed that have identified the special needs individual as one deserving identification for educational funds.

Vocational special needs were identified and funded in the 1968 Amendments to the Vocational Education Act of 1963. Following this law, the Rehabilitation Act of 1973 was passed, providing services to individuals with severe handicapping disabilities. Public Law 93-516 added amendments to the 1973 Act which included equitable service to those who are blind or have impaired sight. In 1978, Public Law 95-602 again amended the 1973 Act to coordinate services among other funding sources for the special needs population.

In 1975 the Education for All Handicapped Children Act defined those characteristics which identify a handicapped individual. The Vocational Education Amendments of 1976 continued the same definition of handicapped as the 1975 Act, but added the following language: "and who, because of their handicapping condition, cannot succeed in the regular vocational education program without special education assistance or who require a modified vocational education program."[6]

The Carl D. Perkins Vocational Education Act of 1984 is again consistent with prior vocational legislation. Part A of this law requires states to spend 57 percent of the state grant for vocational education opportunities for six special populations—handicapped, disadvantaged, adult training and retraining, single parents and homemakers, sex equity, and criminal offenders.

ASSESSING BUSINESS EDUCATION FOR HIGH-RISK POPULATIONS

Since the early 1960's the federal government has provided funds to help education meet the needs of high-risk populations. It is imperative that business educators recruit special populations and train them for careers in business occupations.

Equal access in programming. Business educators must examine their programs and the workplace to identify the many job opportunities available for all individuals who are interested in business courses, but they also must help identify jobs that are available for high-risk students. Because the high-risk students will have many varied backgrounds, an individual assessment of each student must be made cooperatively by the classroom teacher, the counselors, and the administration of a school system. By working together educators in a school system can begin to identify high-risk students who would benefit from courses in business education.[7]

---

[6]Reed, Jack C. "Using a Team Approach When Mainstreaming Special Needs Students." *Business Education Forum* 41:3-4; April 1987.

[7]Sabatino, David A., and Mann, Lester. *A Handbook of Diagnostic and Prescriptive Teaching.* Rockville, MD: Aspen Publishers, 1982.

Students who are identified should be recruited by the teacher and counselor and helped to set goals for a career in business. A study conducted in Chicago found "that students who have goals and students enrolled in career-vocational programs are less likely to drop out than those in traditional school programs."[8]

Once the commitment has been made to work with high-risk individuals, business teachers need to examine their programs and develop strategies for assisting these students to be successful. Weber and Sechler examined nine programs that have been successful with the high-risk population and found the following characteristics present in the nine programs:

- Programs are presented in contexts that differ from a traditional school environment, and they function somewhat autonomously.
- Classrooms have low teacher-pupil ratios.
- Approaches tend to be holistic and multifaceted.
- Strategies are defined by a combination of remedial basic skills, parental involvement, work experience/job placement, counseling, supportive services, and vocational (skill) training.
- Programs focus on students who are in the beginning stages of their high school careers.

Weber and Sechler also found that the staffing of these programs had several things in common, such as ability "to stay on top of their students' needs, to establish relationships with students that tend to be more demanding, and to be committed to their program's philosophy and goals." And, of course, the instruction is devoted to remedial needs, individualization and motivational techniques.[9]

Vocational readiness skills. When working with the high-risk student, the business teacher should be aware of the following learning processes at work in many of these students:

- Learning often takes place at a slower rate and more opportunities for practice will be required.
- Verbal learning provides difficulties, and opportunities for practical experience will give meaning.
- The students may be aged 16-19, they may well be functioning at the level of "concrete operations" in Piagetian terms (mental age 7-11 years) or well below the level of abstract thought.
- There are deficiencies in spontaneous learning which can be overcome by giving structure and direction to the learning.
- Transfer of learning and generalization may be limited and there will be a need to practice new skills in a range of different situations.
- Interest and motivation levels may be difficult to maintain; this can be overcome by providing learning situations which give immediate reinforcement, are relevant, and give direct experience.

[8]Azcoitia, Carlos, and Viso, Philip A. "Dropout Prevention Chicago Style." *Vocational Education Journal* 62:33-34; March 1987.

[9]Weber, James M., and Sechler, Judith A. "Characteristics of Exemplary Vocational Education Programs Designed To Prevent At-risk Youth from Dropping Out." *Educational Leadership* 44:72; March 1987.

- Teaching, by use of familiar situations, self-direction and other methods of independent working, should aim to enhance levels of self-confidence.
- The teacher will need to recognize that many students may be multihandicapped and that problems in the learning situation may have more than one cause.[10]

It is important for the business teacher to present realistic and achievable goals to the high-risk student. However, it is also critical to keep in mind that, if the objectives are too easily attainable, the result may be a lack of motivation on the part of the student. It is necessary to gradually widen a young person's experience to fit in with life in the real world. If this process is managed carefully, perceptions will become more appropriate without the student becoming too discouraged.[11]

Vocational education should build behavior that generalizes across untrained situations and maintains over time without continuous supervision. In developing such work behavior, instruction must address generalization and maintenance issues as well as the initial acquisition of job skills.[12]

INSTRUCTIONAL INTERVENTIONS FOR HIGH-RISK POPULATIONS IN BUSINESS EDUCATION

Assessment of special needs learners. It is important when assessing the high-risk student that the process does not result in a list of negative features detailing what an individual person cannot (or should not) do. The four main criteria for effective assessment may be summarized as follows:

- Parents should be closely involved and contribute to the assessment.
- Aim to discover responses over a period of time and in a variety of settings and not be limited to performance on a single occasion.
- A wide range of professional expertise will be needed if full and appropriate assessment is to be carried out.
- Family and environmental circumstances as a whole will need to be incorporated into the assessment procedures.[13]

Appropriate assessment should call upon a range of expertise, information, and opinion and should not be considered the prerogative of one particular individual or agency. Together these individuals should put together an individualized education plan (IEP) for the student. The teachers, counselors, administrators, psychologists, social workers, and the handicapped young person and his/her family will each have an individual contribution to make. For the best results, vocational assessment should take place on a local basis.

It is important to remember that there are two levels of assessment. The first level includes the *necessary* skills for work, as measured in the form of specific work skills either through test situations or practical work experiences. The other includes the *sufficient* skills for work, in which an attempt

---

[10]Hutchinson, David. *Work Preparation for the Handicapped.* London: Croom Helm Ltd., 1982.

[11]*Ibid.*

[12]Gaylord-Ross, Robert. *Vocational Education for Persons with Handicaps.* Mountain View, CA: Mayfield Publishing Co., 1988.

[13]Hutchinson, *op. cit.*

is made to assess the individual's work personality, indicating his/her strengths and weaknesses as a worker. This assessment can be achieved only through continuing evaluation in a variety of situations during the student's training and work experience. In this way it will be possible to construct a personal profile of each student and to note progressive change.

The objectives of the assessment process should be to establish baselines of performance on which to build and to recognize potential for further development. The profile of abilities and performance of a student can then be used as a check to ensure that the objectives set in the planning of the work program are effectively evaluated, and also as the basis of a report to a potential employer.

Curriculum development for special needs instruction. It is essential to examine the curriculum when working with special needs instruction. Although there are several curriculum development techniques, the functional model and the development model are of greater importance to high-risk populations. The functional model emphasizes the attainment of functional skills—the skills necessary to be successful in a specific environment. Conversely, the developmental model presents skills in a logical sequential manner. Both are appropriate for instruction of special needs, high-risk populations, but critical features must be explored by the teacher in order to ascertain the best model to implement.

Developmental skills include such things as mathematical computations, handwriting, and reading. Most commercially available curriculums contain the normal sequential development of basic skill areas. Typical business education curriculum materials are presented in a developmental format, especially in the skills of keyboarding, shorthand, or accounting. In the basic business courses (general business, economics, and business law), materials produced somewhat follow a developmental curriculum approach. The age of the learner is the most critical factor to determine if this model is most appropriate.[14]

Another drawback is the fact that not all students learn and grow at the same rate. Students' progress is difficult to see with the developmental model. Teachers tend to focus on what a student cannot do as compared to building on what a student can do. Some business subjects must be presented in a patterned way, but high-risk populations generally benefit greater from a functional model.

The terminal goal of the functional model is to equip students with the skills and abilities to succeed in the real world. Much of the standard business education curriculum is functional because the subject deals directly with daily living skills. A functional learning experience should be age-appropriate, utilize the natural environment in which the skills would be performed, and emphasize the content.

A total departure from the developmental approach is not always feasible. Functional curriculum must usually be developed by the classroom teacher because of a lack of commercially prepared materials. Schloss and Sedlak

---

[14]Schloss, P. J., and Sedlak, R. A. *Instructional Methods for Students with Learning and Behavior Problems.* Newton, MA: Allyn and Bacon, 1986.

developed the following process for promoting functional curriculum objectives: identify current and future environments in which the learner is expected to participate; observe others in these settings to determine necessary skills for successful participation; develop a skills checklist that assesses learner competence in using the skills required by the setting; apply the checklist to determine skills the student possesses and skills that are deficit; determine skills that may be accommodated through prosthetics (e.g., calculations, charts, color codes, amplification); delineate developmentally sound task sequences that deal with skill deficits not accommodated through prosthetics; provide educational experiences that promote acquisition of the skill sequences; and assess the learner, using the skills checklist, to determine the effectiveness of instruction and the degree to which the learner is prepared to participate in the target environment.[15]

Special needs, high-risk learners experience great difficulty in acquisition of skills and knowledge when the relevance of the subject matter is not recognized by the learner. Making curriculum functional is one way of assuring that the learner will see the importance of the subject content.

Business education teachers can also serve special needs, high-risk learners successfully by using various curriculum enhancement and modification techniques. It is never the intent to compromise the curriculum requirements but rather to make it more accessible for all types of learners. General areas to examine for enhancing and modifying are learning styles/teaching styles, instructional alternatives, and individualization. Instructional alternatives can further be categorized into classroom organization, classroom management, methods of presentation, methods of practice, and methods of testing.

One of the most effective methodologies to reach special needs, high-risk learners is the employment of learning styles instruments in order to ascertain the student's preferred learning style. Learning style inventories are instruments that indicate the ways in which individuals learn best, the qualities important to people in interacting with others, and the kinds of thinking patterns learners use to solve problems and make decisions.[16] A learning style instrument does not measure knowledge nor does it measure intelligence. The product of the instrument is a personal learning style profile for the student.

The second component of usage of learning style instruments is for each teacher to analyze his/her individual teaching style. This assists the teacher in identifying the appropriate teaching strategy to meet the needs of the high-risk students. Some research shows that teachers tend to teach students in a style that matches the individual teacher's learning style. Teachers should assess their own learning styles, their teaching styles, and the learning styles of individual learners. Once learning styles and teaching styles have been identified, the information can be used to plan the most appropriate instructional methodology to use in the classroom.

---

[15]*Ibid.*

[16]Sarkees, M. D., and Scott, J. L. *Vocational Special Needs.* Second edition. Homewood, IL: American Technical Publishers, 1985.

A number of instructional alternatives are available for the classroom teacher to provide individualization. First, the business educator can vary the organization of the classroom. This can be accomplished by using different types of grouping arrangements such as large- or small-group instruction, peer tutoring, learning centers, or independent self-instructional activities. Also teacher- or student-directed instruction can vary the organization of the classroom.

Another major area of importance to consider is classroom management. This can include varying the grading systems, reinforcement systems, and the rules system. Many times schoolwide policies dictate these decisions; however, it is quite common knowledge that the individual teacher's personality plays an essential role in these areas.

Presenting the content to reach each learner in the classroom is one of the biggest challenges faced by business educators. The methods of presentation can be varied by content, general structure, and type. The amount of content to be learned, the time frame the learner will have, and the conceptual level of the information are variables which can be adjusted to assist the high-risk learner. General structure of the presentation such as previewing questions, giving cues, providing immediate feedback, and actively involving students should be emphasized during the lesson. In the age of high technology in media, the content can no longer be presented just in textbook form. All methods such as verbal-lecture discussion, worksheets, demonstration, videotapes, transparencies, and television must be utilized in every unit if not every lesson.

Methods of practice and testing can also give another opportunity for the classroom teacher to have alternatives for instruction. The type of response and materials can be varied. More than the traditional written test needs to be incorporated into the instruction process. Just as all students do not learn the same way, they cannot be expected to be evaluated in the same manner. The high-risk population should be provided as many opportunities as possible to succeed.

Not all concerns of high-risk learners can be solved through examination and change of the curriculum. The other area which plays an equally essential part in the learning process is the instruction itself. An instructional methodology which is favored by much recent writing and research is direct instructional procedures.

Direct instruction. Direct instruction—including precision teaching, task-analytic instruction, diagnostic teaching, and applied behavior analysis instruction—is characterized by specific instructional procedures.[17] These can be described as assessing learner characteristics, establishing instructional goals, systematic planning of instruction, using instructional materials, using replicable instructional approaches, using motivating consequences, and monitoring student success.

Direct instruction is similar to behavior modification but it focuses specifically on the instructional process. Advocates of direct instruction stress a

---

[17]Schloss and Sedlak, *op. cit.*

logical analysis of the concept to be taught, rather than the characteristics of the student.[18]

Precision teaching enables teachers to become more efficient and effective in adapting their style of teaching to meet the needs of each student in the classroom. This is accomplished by evaluating what is being done and to what level of success students are achieving. Precision teaching requires that teachers be willing to adapt and modify strategies according to student needs.

Task-analytic instruction involves breaking down complex behaviors into their component parts or skill. The teacher develops the first component skill until a success criterion is achieved, then initiates instruction on the second skill, linking it to the previously mastered response. After the second criterion is met, the third one is introduced. This chaining process is continued until all component criteria are achieved. The success of this method is closely tied to the teacher's ability to recognize when a criterion is achieved on one component skill and a second skill can be introduced.[19]

Diagnostic teaching is concerned with the implementation of individualized learning programs for each student. An example of this technique is the usage of IEP's in the field of special education. A requirement for this approach is assessment of the student's present level and specification of goals and objectives.

The basic principle of applied behavior analysis instruction is that it stresses manipulating antecedent and subsequent events to change behavior.[20] Within this system, one will find the major features of a measurement system, precision teaching, instructional aims, and learning principles. It can be easily compared to behavior modification. Therefore, it focuses on reinforcement and punishment.

A summary of direct instruction can be found in the following nine principles which are critical to a successful instructional program for special needs, high-risk learners:

1. Teach one thing at a time.

2. Provide students with multiple opportunities to respond to each lesson.

3. Reinforce students for correct responses throughout the lesson.

4. Correct errors immediately by reteaching through a response paradigm.

5. Review each lesson at the beginning, middle, and end.

6. Keep the pace of interaction quick and "rhythmic."

7. Signal clearly (let students know when lessons begin and when they are expected to respond).

8. Give students opportunities to respond verbally and physically; and

9. Keep the process interactive.[21]

---

[18]Hallahan, D. P., and Kauffman, J. M. *Exceptional Children: Introduction to Special Education.* Fourth edition. Englewood Cliffs, NJ: Prentice Hall, 1988. p. 136.

[19]Schloss and Sedlack, *op. cit.*

[20]Mercer, C. D. *Students With Learning Disabilities.* Second edition. Columbus, OH: A. Bell & Howell Co., 1983.

[21]White, S. "The Modification of Curriculum and Instruction: Catalysts for Equity." *Handbook of Vocational Special Needs Education.* (Edited by G. D. Meers.) Rockville, MD: Aspen Publishers, 1987. pp. 137-60.

Several educational approaches need to be considered when designing special needs instruction. All curriculums and instruction can be enhanced or modified to meet individual learning needs. The challenge of modifying curriculums and instruction is enormous, and it will not be accomplished overnight with any quick fix methods, or even with single instructional formats such as direct instruction.

Business educators need to view the process as ongoing and plan for its implementation when possible. Some traditional educational principles will need to change before teacher autonomy within the classroom can dictate how and what content/curriculum will be presented. The need for enhancing and modifying can easily be justified when it results in effective training for successful employment for special needs, high-risk students.

EVALUATION OF HIGH-RISK POPULATIONS IN BUSINESS EDUCATION

The correct use of evaluation can result in the most appropriate vocational training and placement environment. Vocational educators must rely on community-relevant and community-referenced measures of performance. Job inventories have served as useful tools for evaluating the skills of students and adults with disabilities and then directing appropriate intervention at performance deficits. In the inventory process, a job is analyzed according to the way in which it is performed by a nondisabled worker. Then, evaluation proceeds as follows: (1) A worker with a disability is observed performing the target job in a specific work environment; (2) discrepancies in performance are noted; (3) strategies for increasing skills are developed; and (4) adaptations are developed for skills that the disabled worker is unlikely to acquire. This process allows ongoing evaluation of the worker in the environment in which the job is required.[22]

Evaluation in vocational education can be accomplished by using a combination of testing devices. These may include on-the-job evaluation, work samples, psychometrics, and the IEP.

In the case of on-the-job evaluation, the teacher will be evaluating numerous factors such as how well the student relates to others on the job, listens to and follows instructions from a supervisor, adjusts to a set work schedule, and deals with the stress of extra environmental factors such as noise and activity. Observing how the student performs in relation to how the other workers perform and analyzing what progress the student makes will help in the evaluation process.

Work samples may be obtained from commercial sources or may be written by the teacher. Many commercial work samples provide normative data as well as information on validity and reliability. They are generally comprised of work activities which may attempt to simulate the complete range of activities for a single job, or they may provide selected activities designed to represent a number of related jobs. Work samples are particularly useful

---

[22]McCray, Paul M. *Vocational Evaluation and Assessment in School Settings*. Stout: University of Wisconsin, Research and Training Center, 1982.

101

vocational evaluation tools since they allow the evaluators to assess important work-related characteristics of the student outside of an actual work setting. Work samples, supplemented by on-the-job evaluation techniques, provide a highly effective means of assessing student capabilities.

Locally developed work samples can also provide an excellent means of evaluation because they will often be more closely tied to the demands and limitations of the local labor market than commercially developed work sample systems.

A third type of evaluation test is referred to as psychometrics. There are a number of these tests commonly used in vocational evaluation programs. (A list of these can be found in the publication *Psychological Testing in Vocational Evaluation,* which is available from the Materials Development Center, University of Wisconsin-Stout, Menomonie, WI 54751.)

A fourth method of evaluation is often conducted through the IEP. The team which prepares the plan periodically checks the student's progress to see if the objectives are being met. The group outlines special steps to assist the student in reaching the performance goals in the time allotted.

TRANSITION AND JOB PLACEMENT OF HIGH-RISK POPULATIONS

Transition models and components. One of society's major expectations of schools is that the educational system will prepare students for entry into the world of work and self-sufficiency, which will enable young adults to support themselves. When young adults fail to find gainful employment or to be self-sufficient, society concludes that schools have failed.[23] Business educators recognize that the true success measure of programming is job placement and job retention; business educators want to prepare these students with the skills and abilities needed to obtain gainful employment. The concept of transition from school to work is a relatively new one, and many different components are found in its contents.

Historically, Madelene Will brought transition to national attention as Secretary for the Office of Special Education and Rehabilitation Services (OSERS) in 1984. By making transition a national priority, Will's initiative caused educators to examine their traditional approach to educating high-risk populations and in the process caused a reevaluation of secondary programming for this population. Also, Will defined the process of transition as "a bridge between the security and structure offered by school and the many responsibilities and choices of adult life."[24] Transition is a shared responsibility of all involved parties—student, teacher, vocational counselor, parent, and employer. It has been conceptualized as a process of movement through life's phases. This process encompasses activities that lead to independent living, employment, and other productive life situations.[25]

---

[23]West, L. L. "Designing, Implementing, and Evaluating Transition Programs." *The Journal of Vocational Special Needs,* Volume 11, Number 1, 1988. pp. 3-7.

[24]*Ibid.*

[25]Berkell, D., and Gaylord-Ross, R. "The Concept of Transition: Historical and Current Developments." *Transition from School to Work for Persons with Disabilities.* (Edited by Berkell & J. M. Brown.) White Plains, NY: Longman Inc., 1989. pp. 1-17.

The business educator's role in transition can take on many different functions. Overall, an instructor's role is not to be satisfied with traditional teaching practices such as teaching straight content and acceptable school behavior. Business educators need to infuse skills, experiences, and discussion opportunities that will ultimately give the student the necessary skills to move through all aspects of transition processes throughout all levels of curriculum. Teachers are the key to the development of understanding, examination skills, and strategies concerning transition in an environment that encourages this behavior.[26]

Job placement. One of the major goals of transition for high-risk students is gainful employment. Job placement can be met in three different ways: competitive, supported, or sheltered. Generally the sheltered employment option is not appropriate for business and office occupations and tasks; therefore, only the other two options need to be considered.

Competitive employment is the ultimate goal for special needs, high-risk students. But it is a fact that all students cannot successfully hold a competitive, gainful position. It is for this reason that supported work is now being advocated more frequently for special needs individuals.

Supported employment is defined as competitive work in an integrated work setting for individuals who, because of their handicap, need ongoing services to perform that work. Through such supported employment, persons may receive the necessary services and assistance to learn specific job skills and develop interpersonal and other job-related skills. With the combination of competitive employment and ongoing services, supportive employment provides an opportunity that is rewarding, both personally and professionally, to the high-risk individual.

Prior to job placement or as part of job placement, an effective strategy is the concept of on-the-job training/experience. This can be invaluable to the business educator in developing needed competencies in students to perform specific jobs. Furthermore, when utilizing the work environment, it is quite easy to achieve a functional approach to instruction. Of course, this is the most appropriate approach for special needs, high-risk students. On-the-job training can be used with either the competitive or supported work goal.

Transition does not happen by itself. All participants (i.e., student, teacher, resource personnel, parents, employer, etc.) must take a responsible role to assure its completion. With this team effort, a well-developed transition plan for special needs, high-risk populations will be much more likely to gain positive results.

SUMMARY

Business education teachers are part of the rapidly changing field of vocational training and placement for high-risk students. Instead of being

---

[26]Retish, P. "Educators' Roles in the Transition Process." *Transition From School to Work for Persons with Disabilities.* (Edited by D. E. Berkell & J. M. Brown.) White Plains, NY: Longman Inc., 1989. pp. 108-24.

responders to the concerns of parents and others, business educators must look toward the future and curriculums must include knowledge of critical values and techniques for evaluation, training, placement, and community agency communications and coordination. Educators must include curriculum changes in personnel preparation programs that will result in an increasing number of experts who look beyond traditional in-school and in-class instruction to providing meaningful work opportunities for all students and adults in integrated community businesses and industries.

Business educators can help the high-risk population by taking time to generate recruitment strategies, develop programs, and provide opportunities for actual work experience. Business educators need to take the lead in extending a helping hand to the high-risk students in our schools.

CHAPTER 10

Internationalizing Education
For and about Business

WANDA BLOCKHUS

San Jose State University, San Jose, California

Two hundred years ago Adam Smith observed that specialization and international exchange promote the wealth of nations. Over the past 40 years, four unique phenomena have facilitated international trade—transportation, communications, technology, and language.

Following World War II the United States was the undisputed leader in world trade. It had come through WW II with its continental borders unscarred while many parts of Europe and Asia were devastated. Pent-up demand for consumer goods meant just about everything that could be produced could be sold. Over time Europe and Asia rebuilt and established their own niches in the world marketplace, and now the United States shares leadership with Europe and Asia.

Transportation. Faster and larger planes and lower air fares have enabled more people to move about the globe. You can reach almost any spot in the world within 24 hours. Not only do people travel but so do goods. Some of the clothes and shoes you wear daily come from places halfway around the world, places like Brazil and Korea.

Communications. Communications networks have shrunk the world. News of an earthquake, plane crash, or terrorist attack reaches people around the world via satellites as quickly as those nearby. It is as easy to dial a phone number in Frankfurt or Cape Town or Hong Kong as it is to phone your friend next door. Soon you may regularly dial a toll-free, 800-equivalent number to reach companies on six continents.

Technology. Since World War II, technology has literally changed the way we do business. It has given us television and the accompanying ads. It has given us microchips and computers, men on the moon, aseptic packaging, and cures for diseases like polio. It has also brought people up close and personal. We have seen in living horror the space shuttle disaster and little children starving in third world countries.

Language. A common language helps facilitate international business. Since World War II, English has supplanted French as the common language. English is now the language of business; for example, English is the language used in control towers around the world at airports handling international flights. The United Nations has six official languages representing the most used languages in the world: English, Spanish, French, Chinese, Russian, and

105

Arabic. In many parts of the world, it is common now to see signs with more than one language, or packaging with three or four languages. Street signs in Japan Town in San Francisco are in English and Japanese; in China Town, in English and Chinese. Signs in the Tokyo underground are in Japanese and English. Signs in a fashionable California department store elevator are in English and Italian. Many American cities have Spanish names, such as Los Angeles, San Antonio, and Palo Alto. Even though people may use English as a common language, they remain loyal to their native tongue. This is readily apparent as you listen to passengers talking with one another at international airports.

EDUCATION FOR AND ABOUT INTERNATIONAL BUSINESS

Business education's traditional goals have been to prepare students to enter and advance in jobs within business, and to prepare them to handle their own business affairs and function intelligently in a business economy. Those goals have not changed. What has changed is the rise in importance in international business. Even though most students will not work in a foreign country or even travel outside the United States, they still are a part of a vast international marketplace. They may work for companies which export goods, and they most certainly will buy and use goods from around the world.

UNITED STATES EXPORTS

Canada, Japan, Mexico, the United Kingdom, and West Germany share the distinction of being the leading foreign markets for products exported from the United States in 1987. At the same time, Japan, Canada, West Germany, Taiwan, Mexico, the United Kingdom, and South Korea were the leading countries from which the United States imported goods.

What kinds of goods does the United States export? The capital goods sector leads exports, followed by industrial supplies and materials, foods, feeds, beverages, and automotive products. About 2000 companies account for more than 70 percent of exports.

And who are the exporters? General Motors, Ford Motor, and Boeing were the top three American firms in foreign sales in a recent year. Rounding out the top ten were General Electric, IBM, E.I. Du Pont de Nemours, McDonnell Douglas, Chrysler, Eastman Kodak, and Caterpillar.

Forty-eight percent of Prime Computer's sales were exports, as was 41 percent of Boeing's sales. Intel exported 28 percent of its sales; Caterpillar, 27 percent; McDonnell Douglas, 25 percent; Ethyl, 22 percent; Digital Equipment, 21 percent; Hewlett-Packard, 20 percent; FMC, 20 percent; and Motorola, 19 percent. Sales figures alone give an incomplete picture. What about profit? In a recent year Exxon earned 59 percent of its profits from foreign sales; IBM, 47 percent; and Polaroid, 61 percent. As for number of employees, some companies employ more than half of their work force outside the United States. For example, Johnson & Johnson has 57 percent of its employees outside the U.S. and Ford Motor has 53 percent outside. International business is a vital part of sales as this data shows.

UNITED STATES IMPORTS

Just as American companies are eager to market abroad, so foreign companies are eager to market in the United States. Four qualifications are necessary to have a market, domestic or foreign. They are: (1) people, (2) with money to spend, (3) willingness to spend it, and (4) authority to buy.

The United States is a very attractive market. It has a population of over 244 million and per capita income of $18,200. Some other countries are more populous than the United States and others have higher per capita incomes, but it is the combination of population and income which attracts marketers from abroad. Certain products which Americans buy everyday are made by foreign companies, such as Nestle's chocolate chips and coffee, Toyota and BMW automobiles, Sony television sets, Shell gasoline, and Lux dishwashing products. The United States depends on foreign countries for many unbranded products, too, such as cut flowers, fruits, and vegetables.

Industrial companies engage in manufacturing or mining. The 10 largest industrials outside the United States in a recent year included:

1. Royal Dutch/Shell Group, The Hague/London
2. British Petroleum, London
3. IRI, Rome
4. Toyota Motor, Toyota City, Japan
5. Daimier-Benz, Stuttgart
6. Matsushita Electric Industrial, Osaka
7. Volkswagen, Wolfsburg, West Germany
8. Hitachi, Tokyo
9. ENI, Rome
10. Philips' Gloeilampenfabrieken, Eindhoven, Netherlands

AMERICA'S TRADING PARTNERS

Envision world trade as a triangle with America at one apex, Europe at another, and East Asia at the third. The European Economic Community (EEC) includes Belgium, Denmark, France, Great Britain, Greece, Ireland, Italy, Luxembourg, the Netherlands, Portugal, Spain, and West Germany. East Asian countries include Australia, Indonesia, Japan, Malaysia, New Zealand, Papua New Guinea, Philippines, South Korea, Taiwan, and Thailand.

In 1987 the United States exported $67 billion to the European Economic Community and $69 billion to East Asia. In turn, the United States imported $85 billion from the EEC and $158 billion from East Asia. The EEC exported $50 billion to East Asia, and East Asia exported $80 billion to the EEC.

Two countries with major resources of people and land are not covered in this data. The People's Republic of China and the Soviet Union are presently making major changes in political and economic policies. No doubt over the next 25 years, we will see major shifts in international trading as both countries develop their interest and ability to be major players in world trade.

The ten most populous countries of the world (in order) are People's Republic of China, India, the Soviet Union, the United States, Indonesia, Brazil, Japan, Bangladesh, Nigeria, and Pakistan. All have many people, some have great economic wealth, some have land and other natural resources, and others, military power. Some are impoverished and still struggling just to feed the population.

In 1987 selected countries of the world shared the world's gross national product in this proportion: United States, 26 percent; European Economic Community, 22 percent; Soviet Union, 14 percent; Japan, 9 percent; Eastern Europe, 5 percent; the People's Republic of China, 2 percent; and others, 22 percent.

In looking at a market in terms of potential, the country's economic growth rate is another variable, in addition to the gross national product. Over the last decade, the Soviet Union, the European Economic Community, and Japan experienced a decrease in their annual growth rate; the United States' growth rate remained almost constant; and the People's Republic of China had a dramatic increase.

Let us look at selected countries on several criteria.

World Players in the Game of Economics

	U.S.	U.S.S.R.	Japan	EEC	China
Population in millions	244	284	122	324	1,074
GNP (1987 US $)	$ 4,436	$2,375	$ 1,608	$ 3,782	$ 295
Per capita GNP	$18,200	$8,360	$13,180	$11,690	$ 270
GNP 1987 growth rate	2.9%	.5%	4.2%	2.9%	9.4%
Agriculture Production Kilograms per capita					
Grain	1150	740	130	480	402
Meat	109	65	31	82	18
Military—Active Armed Forces in millions	2,163	5,096	245	2,483	3,200

MAJOR CHANGES IN INTERNATIONAL BUSINESS IN THE 1990'S

Canada. By 1998 all United States-Canada trade is to be duty free. The United States exports more goods to Canada than to any other country; and Canada is second after Japan as the source of imports. Trade between these two neighbors will be further facilitated as a result of legislation passed by the U.S. Congress and by the Canadian Parliament in 1988. Prime Minister Brian Mulroney spearheaded what may be Canada's most important economic decision this century. For Canadians, his leadership signaled the removal of all trade barriers over the next ten years.

Tariffs on goods such as computers, whiskey, needles, vending machines, skis, skates, and frozen food were removed in 1989. Other tariffs were reduced as part of a five to ten year phase-out. Border procedures were relaxed in 1989 to allow businessmen greater freedom to travel back and forth across the United States-Canadian border. Two of the first American industries to benefit from the relaxed trade barriers were expected to be telecommunications and financial service companies.

Negotiations were begun in 1989 to establish new rules to govern: (1) anti-dumping, a situation where duties are imposed when goods are sold on export markets at lower than domestic market prices; (2) countervailing duties which are imposed on goods to offset benefits from subsidies; and (3) trade-related subsidies.

European Economic Community. A single European market of 300 million people rivaling the United States and Japan will be created in 1992. Twelve European countries will become a single market via removal of physical, fiscal, and technical barriers to trade. People, products, and services will be able to move among EEC nations as easily as they cross state borders within the United States. Technical, health, and safety requirements will be standardized. N.V. Philips was just one company that called for standardization for consumer electronics. Multinational marketers envision one advertising program instead of 12 separate ones. Certain products, such as Colgate toothpaste, will be offered as a single formula rather than regional. Johnson & Johnson, MasterCard International, and Johnson Wax are three of many companies realigning products and advertising directed to a single market instead of multiple European markets.

What may have been thought of as a single act of unification was an array of 300 directives from the EEC headquarters in Brussels. Such legislation impacted just about every industry. Some formerly protected markets, such as state-subsidized airline companies, state broadcasting monopolies, and state oil and gas monopolies, will be competing not only with companies within their own country but also with companies within the EEC and companies overseas. Such industries see diversification as one way to compete.

The removal of these trade barriers may prove a bonanza for small companies which formerly had to limit their marketing to their own region. New brands will enter the market, and some brands will disappear. For example, the Swiss multinational, Nestle, formerly sold yogurt in West Germany under three regional brands but is expected to drop two of those brands by 1992. A single monetary unit for the 12 countries has been discussed but not with much enthusiasm.

The Soviet Union. Nowhere in the world are there such sweeping changes in economic policy as in the Soviet Union. In a few short years the Russian word, "perestroika," has entered the vocabulary of people around the world. Simply put, perestroika is the Soviet blueprint for economic reform designed to make Russia competitive in world trade. The architect of perestroika, Abel Aganbegyan, the chief economic adviser to Soviet President Mikhail Gorbachev, told the World Forum of Silicon Valley in 1988 that, "Perestroika is the fate of our nation."

President Gorbachev initiated sweeping changes to restructure the Soviet Union's political, social, and economic orientation. The Soviet Union has over 280 million people with a per capita income of $8400. Russia has a well established military machine supported by 16 percent of the country's GNP.

However, it is hampered by a populace which lacks a tradition of economic enterprise or individual initiative.

In order to be a leader in world business, a country needs money, market size, and more. It needs power derived from a combination of military, political, economic, and cultural clout, including the intangibles that make a nation admired and respected. Mr. Aganbegyan acknowledged in San Jose as he also did to audiences in New York, Chicago, and Los Angeles that the Soviet Union's policies regarding agriculture, housing, education, consumer goods, and other sectors simply have not worked. The average Soviet citizen still spends his days standing in lines with the inevitable plastic sack seeking to buy essentials such as food and clothing, and yearning for consumer goods such as TV sets and VCR's.

Although it will take time, certain reforms are being put in place such as joint ventures between the United States and other countries, major reforms in foreign and economic trade activities, free economic zones in coastal and inland areas to promote trade, and a plan to make the Soviet currency convertible. The most challenging aspect of perestroika and one that will take the longest to achieve—is convertible currency.

The People's Republic of China. Not only are there major economic changes in North America, the European Community, and the Soviet Union, but a most significant change in another part of the world will take place in 1997 when Hong Kong will revert from Great Britain to the People's Republic of China.

After being closed for some 30 years, China opened its doors some 10 years ago. Enormous changes are taking place in Hong Kong as it prepares to revert to China, one of which is the well publicized brain drain and moving of money to other parts of the world. The prospect of 1997 has not appeared to slow growth at all in Hong Kong. New construction is readily apparent, and labor shortages continue.

Hong Kong industry has crept across the border into China. In a recent year it was estimated that Hong Kong companies employ about 1.5 million people in Guangdong Province, or about twice the 850,000 manufacturing employees in Hong Kong itself. In 1988 for the first time re-exports, or shipments of goods through Hong Kong (mainly to and from China), exceeded the total value of domestic exports from Hong Kong.

Hong Kong will likely become a service center for the economy of Southern China. Likely it will provide value-added services to products manufactured in the interior, services such as banking, trade, financing, accounting, legal services, design, marketing, tourism, and even manufacturing.

China, like Russia, has embarked on economic overhaul. Unlike Russia, China's reform is singular—economic only, while Russia is assaulting political and social fronts as well. China is more likely to join the world economy in the decades ahead; for one thing, China has generations of experience with commerce, and even though suppressed for 30 years, the instincts are still there.

China's reform is clearly focused on economics. The debate in China is not over whether to reform, but rather on how to reform. One representative of the Academy of Social Sciences in Beijing went so far as to say that the only economic theory that works is the market theory; it has proven its strength and can't be put into the bottle again.

ENVIRONMENTAL FORCES IN INTERNATIONAL BUSINESS

Doing business across national boundaries is different from doing business at home. The business environment consists of external forces that directly or indirectly influence the success of doing business abroad. These environmental forces include economic, political and legal, cultural, social, and technological factors.

Economic. Before entering a foreign market, a company would consider data such as total personal income, per capita income, income distribution, disposable income, discretionary income, distribution of wealth, availability of consumer credit, availability of capital, and rate of savings. It would be folly to consider only one economic indicator, for example, total personal income. Even though total personal income may be high for a country such as India, it may be a poor indicator of market potential because of India's large population. Per capita income should be considered along with total personal income.

Opportunities for international marketers are not limited to those countries with the highest incomes. Countries such as the People's Republic of China, Mexico, and Greece may be good potential markets for certain products.

Political and legal. A country's laws and its political system have great impact on international business. Some countries require that 50 percent ownership of an enterprise must be held within the country. Some countries have rigid tariff barriers in order to protect their own markets. The political stability of a country may be the major factor in entering or not entering that country. The political instability of some countries, some African nations and some Central and South American countries, may force a company to abandon or defer marketing there. A company would not want to invest capital equipment in a country if there is the possibility that industry will be nationalized.

Cultural. Culture is a handed-down way of life. It may include concepts and values as well as tangibles such as architecture, tools, and food. Body language, colors, and symbols may have very different meanings from one country to another. Older people are revered in Eastern cultures, while youth is honored in the West. Using income and expenditures as criteria, education is much more highly honored in Japan than in the United States.

Bowing is the traditional form of greeting in Japan, while in India the palms of the hands are placed together and the head is nodded. In Latin America, the traditional form of greeing is a hearty embrace followed by a friendly slap on the back. In the Middle East, the word "no" must be mentioned three times before it is accepted.

The business customs regarding male-female social interaction vary from country to country. Advertising based on the togetherness of married life might not be appropriate in Western Europe since husbands and wives tend to lead separate lives. In the Orient, commercials portraying romantic love are unacceptable.

Americans make mistakes abroad, and foreigners make mistakes in America. For example, Braniff Airlines designed commercials in Spanish to highlight the leather seats in aircraft. Unfortunately, the literal translation of the commercials was an invitation to fly naked. Brand names acceptable in Japan were not appropriate for the American market—products such as Calpis, Pocket Wetty hand towels, and a soft drink called Pocari Sweat. Coined names or names without meaning, perhaps, are the best of all, for example, the coined name *Exxon.* The name *Sony* came from the Latin word *sonus* meaning sound, which reflected the company's early product—tape recorders. It is short, easy to remember, and easy to pronounce.

Social forces. Attitudes toward family, education, health, recreation, religion, and other institutions affect behavior in the marketplace. Wedding celebrations vary greatly, ranging from five-day festivities to a simple ceremony before a state official. Some countries, such as Australia, place great value on leisure time and athletic events.

Interest in sports varies from country to country. American football is not popular in Europe or Asia, but European football, or soccer, is popular around the world. Devotion to soccer in places such as Ireland and Brazil approaches national hysteria. In other countries, people feel the same about cricket.

Women are accepted and encouraged in the workplace in America, but this is not true of all countries of the world. One Silicon Valley firm lost its chance to do business in Japan because it sent a hard-hitting young woman executive to Japan to negotiate. Her manner of doing business in the U.S. was just not acceptable in Japan, and she could not change centuries of social practice in one week's visit. The old cliche is true: When in Rome, do as the Romans do.

Technology. Export of technology of strategic importance to the United States may require approval of the U.S. Department of Defense before foreign sales can be approved. Military equipment, scientific equipment, computers, and jet engines may fall into this category.

World standards would facilitate marketing across national boundaries, for example, standardizing electrical outlets. Beta video tape became obsolete when VHS was finally adopted as the standard. Computer diskettes are made in three formats, and disks for Apple computers are not generally compatible with IBM equipment. Until there are universal standards, companies must pay close attention to the specifications of the countries where they plan to market.

WAYS TO ENTER INTERNATIONAL MARKETS

The simplest way to enter international markets is by exporting. The product is not changed, and there is little or no attention paid to promotion and distribution. Pricing may only cover the cost of the product without research and development costs, making the product less expensive abroad than at home.

Licensing is another way to enter international markets. Companies such as Coca Cola and Pepsi Cola license firms in the Soviet Union, or the People's Republic of China, or scores of other countries, to produce their soft drinks. With licensing, there is no direct investment in the country. The licensee pays commissions on sales or supplies used.

A joint venture is a partnership between a domestic firm and a foreign firm or government. Joint ventures operate in many countries of the world and are especially popular in industries which require large investments. A huge auto assembly plant, the New United Motors, (NUMI), is a joint venture between General Motors and Toyota in Fremont, California. The United States and Saudi Arabian joint ventures have proven to be popular in large construction projects in Saudi Arabia. The Soviet Union has entered into joint ventures with companies in the United Kingdom and West Germany.

A fourth way of doing international business is by direct ownership of a foreign subsidiary or division. Here there is a big commitment to manufacturing equipment and personnel. The wholly owned subsidiary may be allowed to operate independently of the parent company.

TEACHING-LEARNING STRATEGIES FOR INTERNATIONAL BUSINESS

Business students at all levels should attain at least a minimal level of competency in international business. A 1986 survey of collegiate business school curriculums shows that most schools do offer study in the international dimension. The most-offered course was an international marketing course; about two-thirds of the undergraduate and graduate business schools offered an international marketing course. Secondary schools are unlikely to offer a separate course; however, the international dimension can be integrated into existing courses. Here are some ways.

Reports. Students in almost any business class can be given the assignment to do a report on an aspect of international business. Topics might include a general country report or a multinational company report, or a more specific topic such as business customs in Scandinavia. Several students might prepare individual reports on Norway, Denmark, Sweden, and Finland and then together present a panel discussion on Scandinavia.

Students who are oriented more to field-type research than library research might be assigned to go to a grocery store for a particular category of goods to determine those made by foreign companies. Or, they might be asked to find in the grocery store as many foreign produced goods as they can in a 15-minute period. The research could be done in a department store or clothing store as well. Students might be assigned a particular magazine, such as *Sports Illustrated* or *Seventeen*, to list all the ads and then identify the ads of foreign companies. Depending on the lead time for the report, students could write to an American company for an annual report and then prepare a report on the multinational aspects of the company.

Students in the class who were born or lived in another country or who have traveled abroad could be invited to give a first-hand account on marketing in that country. Such accounts tend to be informative and entertaining. For example, Americans buy eggs from refrigerated cases, but not so in other parts of the world. If you ask for a fresh chicken in some countries, the clerk goes out back and rings the neck off the chicken. In Western Europe, catsup and mustard are packaged in tubes not unlike toothpaste. Some countries have set prices; in others, you are expected to bargain for the price.

The business resource center could build a collection of foreign language magazines and newspapers and the ads could be analyzed. Examples of foreign currency could be collected. Comparative prices for a particular item—a Big Mac, a T-shirt, or a television set—could be determined by converting the price to foreign currencies, using exchange rates published in newspapers.

Students could research requirements for visiting selected countries, including such things as whether a visa is required, how passports and visas are obtained, and what to do if a passport is lost or stolen. Students who are artistic might prepare posters, bulletin boards, or other visual displays on international topics. If students are given enough advance notice, they can usually get postcards or store sacks from points outside the country. These make very interesting discussion points as well as displays.

Students could be assigned one Sunday edition of a local paper to clip all stories having to do with anything international. The results will include stories of politics, sports stars from abroad, and stories about world business.

A committee of interested students could brainstorm other activities relating to international business. Students may have traveled abroad as exchange students or members of sports teams, choirs, or church groups, and their input would be especially useful.

Students could research various exchange programs for students and perhaps locate adults who have been on such exchanges and invite them to class to speak. Other speakers might include Americans who have worked abroad, or foreign nationals who are now working in the United States.

Resources. The popular film, "Going International," produced by Copeland Griggs, 411 15th Avenue, San Francisco, CA 94118, is available on film or videotape. Its six parts include segments on bridging the culture gap and managing the overseas assignment. The Enterprise Series on public television has several segments on international business, such as one on the diamond trade and another on Kentucky Fried Chicken going overseas. Students or faculty may present slides of international subjects.

The teacher can build a collection of appropriate books, maps, and reports, either in the library or classroom. Guidebooks or books on international business can be included, such as the following:

Andrus, David M., and others. *International Marketing Management: A Reader.* Bessemer, AL: Colonel Press, 1988.

Chesanow, Neil. *The World Class Executive.* (How to do business like a pro around the world.) New York: Rawson, 1985.

Copeland, Lennie, and Griggs, Lewis. *Going International.* New York: New American Library, 1986.

Harris, Philip R., and Moran, Robert T. *Managing Cultural Differences.* Houston: Gulf Publishing Co., 1988.

Kidron, Michael, and Segal, Ronald. *The New State of the World Atlas.* New York: Simon & Schuster, 1987.

Onkvisit, Sak, and Shaw, John J. *International Marketing, Analysis and Strategy.* Columbus, OH: Merrill Publishing Co., 1989.

Schrag, Adele F., and Poland, Robert P. *A System for Teaching Business Education.* New York: McGraw-Hill Publishing Co., 1987.

Business periodicals such as *Business Week, Fortune,* and the *Wall Street Journal* contain a wealth of current data about international business, as do business sections of major newspapers.

The federal government, some state governments, trade associations, and others regularly publish data about international business. A local librarian can assist in locating such sources.

Part III

FOUNDATIONS OF A SOLID FUTURE FOR BUSINESS EDUCATION

CHAPTER 11

Research for Shaping the Future of Business Education

JUDITH J. LAMBRECHT
University of Minnesota, St. Paul

JOLENE D. SCRIVEN
Northern Illinois University, DeKalb

As a body of professional educators, business teachers can claim an assumption about both their distinctiveness and their responsibilities with regard to research. An assumption held by any group which considers itself a distinctive area of study is that the research questions important to the field can best be addressed by members of that professional field, using, when appropriate, the research findings from other more fundamental disciplines. In short, the issues and concerns which affect business education today and the answers to which will shape its future, need to be addressed by reseachers from within the field itself—by business educators. Business educators themselves need to be both competent interpreters of existing research and full participants in the conduct of research.

This chapter looks at the roles of both "users" and "doers" as necessary complements: doing research of substance requires a commitment to critically reviewing existing bodies of knowledge in the field.

USERS OF RESEARCH

Business teachers and administrators at all teaching levels are dependent upon quality research as a basis for the program planning and teaching decisions which they make. Research and ongoing program assessment are the implicit underpinnings of professional education. A key outcome of a professional program is the development of independent learners who can continue to use the resources of a field to guide their actions, upgrade educational programs, and critically assess the educational recommendations which come from many "interested publics." Making use of existing research requires an understanding of the general types of questions which research can answer, knowing where to locate relevant research, and then becoming a critical reader of existing reports.

Types of research. Research questions can be broadly classified as five types: descriptive, associational, experimental, ethnographic or interpretive, and historical. It is important to recognize the kind of question for which

116

each of these research types is appropriate and to recognize the limitations of each type of research for providing guidance.

An expectation in any professional endeavor is that those who act as teachers or administrators believe their actions to be effective; they expect to make a difference by their behavior. They believe that their plans and actions will be effective in reaching identifiable goals. In essence, they rely on implicit cause-and-effect relationships which they believe to exist or conditions which they believe to be true.

Of course, not all actions can be traced to assumptions which are supported by research; if professionals were to seek such support for all their behaviors, they would be paralyzed for action. For many sound and necessary decisions, supporting research would be hard to find. All rational behavior may not have a readily available research base, but important teaching and program-development decisions need research-supported rationales when it becomes apparent that choices exist, problems need to be solved, and costs and effectiveness of alternatives need to be evaluated.

DESCRIPTIVE RESEARCH. Questions about the state of current affairs are the domain of descriptive research. It permits summary statements about the characteristics of given groups of objects—businesses, office workers, schools, students, outcomes from given types of activities, and feelings or judgments on given topics. Descriptive research has been the most common type of research carried out in business education in the last two decades.

Descriptive research is a necessary tool for establishing the state of current employment needs, job requirements, or judgments about the relative importance of different program outcomes. Descriptive research allows professionals to document the outcomes of their programs and to match these outcomes with prior expectations or needs. Descriptive research can be looked upon as both census taking and accountability reporting. It may be the basis for more penetrating questions about the likelihood of occurrence of the characteristics described, their desirability, and potentially, their cause.

The prominence of descriptive research is understandable in a field such as business, which has been markedly altered by technological, social, and economic changes. What is more, the breadth of potential business content areas requires that teachers ask recurrently about the relative importance of given topics and skills. Instructional time is never sufficient to exhaust the potential of most major business content areas. Business teachers need to establish *what* to teach before they can ask *how* most effectively to teach it.

ASSOCIATIONAL RESEARCH. Describing the current state of affairs is seldom sufficient. It has already been suggested that relative degrees of importance can be assigned to curriculum decisions. It is also likely that different types of businesses, schools, student groups, subject areas, teachers, or levels of employees can differ on important issues.

Asking about differences means asking about associations—do groups differ in ways that are related to the category types? If so, might it be possible to anticipate these differences just by knowing the category? Prediction is the desired outcome. If events or objects tend to occur together, knowing one characteristic could mean knowing a second. For example, aptitude testing looks for relationships so that predictions can be made about likely future outcomes. In the past, business educators looked for predictors of academic outcomes in such areas as shorthand and accounting. Today, they seek predictors of broader outcomes—problem-solving ability, critical thinking, transfer to new settings. Some of the predictors include learning style, gender, or specific content preparation, such as programming instruction or computer competencies. It is likely such associational searches will continue to be carried out so that programs can be tailored to respond to the needs of different types of students.

Descriptive data is undoubtedly more meaningful when existing relationships can be identified. Further, when relationships are found to exist, it is inviting to look for a reason. Do events or characteristics just happen to occur together, or is one causing the other? Perhaps the related characteristics are being caused by another unidentified object, event, or characteristic.

The trap of associational research is to infer causal relationships which may not exist. If causal relationships do exist, the relationship will be observed; but the reverse is not necessarily true. Observing a relationship alone cannot be used as proof of cause-effect situations. Sophisticated path-analysis techniques may permit stronger cases for defending causal relationships, but generally the research tool used to establish causation is the experiment.

EXPERIMENTAL RESEARCH. Historically, experimental research has accounted for less than one-third of the graduate-level research in business education. It has been done most often in business content areas with well-established, less volatile subject matter such as bookkeeping/accounting, communications, business math, shorthand/transcription, and keyboarding. Other areas, such as word processing, have become the object of experimental studies after they have been established within the curriculum.

The purpose of experimental studies is to identify causal relationships so that recommendations can be made on a course of action. Alternatively, experimental research may answer, or raise, questions about fundamental relationships that would increase understanding about *why* different approaches are effective. Such explanations might permit generalization beyond the specific subject matter of an experiment. For example, if different copy characteristics can be identified as associated with more or fewer errors, the expectation is that these copy characteristics can be generalized beyond the specific text passages of an experiment. Such knowledge about the causes of errors will affect instructional materials development. Further, if instructional computing software with given characteristics can be shown to be effective, these characteristics may be incorporated into other similar software packages to teach related topics.

ETHNOGRAPHIC OR INTERPRETIVE RESEARCH. Experimental research in educational settings has frequently been called *applied* research, not *basic* research, which has the purpose of advancing fundamental scientific knowledge. In what sense, then, can educational research be said to address fundamental questions? Is this the role only of physical sciences? Basic research in applied fields, such as education, can be considered to be of a different nature than the empirical science endeavor. Rather, a more useful differentiation may be between research which *refines* and that which *reconstructs.*[1]

Research which refines is descriptive, associational, or experimental research which focuses on "doing things right" within the current framework of existing goals, programs, and policies. Reconstructive research, on the other hand, focuses on "doing the right things." It asks about goals, purposes, and meanings and explores the possibility of fundamental changes in the end/means relationships of existing systems.[2]

These are the kinds of questions asked when the place of business education in the public educational systems as a whole is examined. Qualitative, perhaps ethnographic, methods of inquiry can be used to ask about the balance between vocational preparation and general/academic education. By focusing on broader social contexts and personal meanings and interpretations, judgments are made are about the "ends" desired from educational endeavors and hypotheses can be generated for further examination.

HISTORICAL RESEARCH. A small portion of business education research can be considered historical. Frequently this research traces the influence of key individuals in the field, examining their writings or interviewing groups of persons in distinctive groups (award winners) to compare and contrast their perceptions. By studying the past, a better understanding of current institutions, practices, or problems is sought. It could be said that the historical researcher is *discovering* data, while the other research types involve the creation of data. In both instances, the desired outcome is the identification of associations that will increase understanding of events.

Problems in existing research. It is possible to find numerous examples of technical problems which compromise the generalizability of research findings: small sample sizes, lack of random selection of subjects, lack of experimental research in preference to descriptive surveys, failure in experimental studies to describe fully what is meant by the "traditional" methods used, instrumentation problems related to test validity and reliability, and inappropriate procedures. Technical problems are easy to find; they are also relatively easy to correct with appropriate educational preparation of researchers.

More serious problems exist, however, in the nature of the questions being raised by business education research. This is not a problem area easily addressed by a single research course as preparation—it requires depth of understanding about the business problem at hand. Frequently business education research lacks the conceptual development to support the data-collection efforts that are undertaken. The rationale for asking specific questions and the framework through which to interpret the findings is frequently missing, particularly in descriptive studies.

The existence of numerous descriptive studies is not in itself a symptom of a problem. In a field markedly affected by the dynamics of technological

---

[1]Moss, J., Jr. "The Purpose of Reserach in Vocational Education." *Journal of Industrial Teacher Education,* Volume 26, Number 1, 1988. pp. 82-85.

[2]Copa, G. "What Should We Do About Research in Vocational Education?" *Beacon: American Vocational Education Research Association* 10:1-8; Winter 1981.

changes, demographic shifts, and economic trends, current snapshot pictures of the true state of affairs are necessary for intelligent planning. But many of the descriptive studies undertaken fall short of raising a researchable question—namely, a question which includes examination of the relationships among important variables.

Not only do many descriptive studies fail to examine potential relationships among variables, but the questions raised lack justification. Several current surveys report findings about corporate use of computing software and hardware—findings that match the information already known from readily available sales data. Why confirm the obvious over and over? More penetrating questions could be justified about how specific software applications are used by different types of office workers. For example, some studies report that spreadsheets are used by business employees to perform summation and average functions, or even to do accounting. Are there not more probing questions to ask about how spreadsheets are used in order to derive specific curriculum recommendations?

Lack of a sound rationale for the descriptive data collected and lack of well-thought-out reasons for expecting potential relationships between variables mean that the implications of any findings will be hard to identify. Conclusions become, in effect, trivial restatements of study findings.

It is difficult for many researchers to separate conceptually the difference between the *problem* of a study (the question to be answered) and the *purpose* of the study (the reason for asking the question and the expected benefit from obtaining an answer). The purpose of a study must go beyond merely answering the questions posed. And the reason for asking questions must include better justification than merely that some things are interesting to know. Research needs to build on past efforts—extending knowledge and improving upon recognized weaknesses. It is easy to acknowledge how little is known about specific topics, but competent research can be planned only by those who already know much—who have identified the base upon which to build and the holes which need to be filled.

Using existing research. Gaining access to research sources in business education is the first step in using relevant information. The challenge is to search with sufficient breadth so as not to miss relevant thinking from many sources. At the same time, the challenge is also not to become overwhelmed by the information which imposes itself upon decision makers. Within the business education field, research reports are available in several periodicals. Some are designed to apply a synthesis of research findings to practical classroom settings; other are more comprehensive reports of single research projects and frequently appear in refereed journals.

Refereed journals are of particular value for research dissemination to the researcher and the reader because of the peer review which is part of the selection. Competitive review is considered to be one means of substantiating the quality and relevance of the research reported. Nonrefereed periodicals may use invitational and/or volunteer means for acquiring manuscripts. The quality of nonrefereed reports is not necessarily lower than that of reports in refereed publications, but the purpose of the journal is different. Refereed publications are a means of disseminating research in a professional environment which values competitive review as a means for selecting meritorious work. Less formal reports for practitioners frequently focus on theme topics or current problems of interest to a wide audience.

The more practitioner-oriented journals which may report research are the following:

- *Business Education Forum*
- *The Balance Sheet*
- *Business Education World*
- *Business Exchange*
- *Journal of Business Communication*
- *Instructional Strategies: An Applied Research Series* (formerly *TIPS*)
- *Data Base*
- *Journal of Economic Education*
- *Vocational Education Journal.*

In addition to these, other technology-related journals are also likely sources of research reports which affect the teaching of business subjects. Some of these include:

- *The Computing Teacher*
- *Electronic Learning*
- *Educational Technology*
- *Computers and the Social Sciences*
- *Academic Computing*
- *Computers in the Schools*
- *Journal of Artificial Intelligence in Education*
- *T.H.E. Journal.*

Broadly based education-related periodicals should not be overlooked, since frequently these contain research reports impacting business education as well as other subject-matter fields. These include:

- *Harvard Educational Review*
- *Phi Delta Kappan*
- *Educational Leadership*
- *Educational Horizons.*

The refereed periodicals which focus on business education topics include the following:

- *The Delta Pi Epsilon Journal*
- *NABTE Review*
- *Journal of Education for Business*
- *The Journal of Vocational Education Research*
- *Office Systems Research Journal.*

Other refereed, research-focused journals in education which should be included by business education researchers as potential sources include:

- *American Educational Research Journal*
- *Behavior and Information Technology*
- *Cognition and Instruction*
- *Journal of Computer-Based Instruction*
- *Journal of Research on Computing in Education* (formerly the *AEDS Journal*)
- *Journal of Educational Computing Research*
- *Journal of Research and Development in Education*
- *Journal of Educational Psychology*
- *Journal of Educational Research*
- *Review of Educational Research*
- *Review of Research in Education.*

These lists reinforce the breadth of the business education field and its fundamental disciplines but do not include an even longer list of periodicals designed for business professional staff. These periodicals focus explicitly on business content and technology and on training or human resource development from the corporate point of view. They provide current and fundamental background for research related to teaching business subjects at any school level.

In many instances, periodical resources can be a substitute for seeing a complete research report or dissertation. However, for persons developing proposals, access to periodical literature should not supplant acquiring complete research reports. Restrictions on published manuscript length mean that much of the conceptual development and procedural information about a research undertaking is omitted. Extending knowledge in a specific area and benefiting from other researchers' experiences require that complete research reports be consulted on closely related projects.

Finding specific titles of related research requires use of the bibliographic indexes available. The *Business Education Index* published by Delta Pi Epsilon, will provide identification of both teaching- and content-related material. Other essential indexes to use for locating related business literature include the *Business Periodicals Index, Microcomputer Index, Education Index,* and the *Current Index to Journals in Education* (CIJE). The periodical literature in these indexes can be searched on-line in many university libraries. The on-line indexes are called ABI/INFORM for business periodicals, *Microcomputer Index* to parallel the paper version, and *Magazine Index* and *Educational Resources Information Center* (ERIC) for educational titles.

Also available for on-line searching is *Dissertation Abstracts International,* a key source of titles of doctoral research. These titles are also available specifically for business education in a series of publications from Delta Pi Epsilon: *Index to Doctoral Dissertations in Business Education (1900-1975); Supplement, 1975-1980;* and *Supplement, 1980-1985.* Abstracts of selected doctoral dissertations in business education are available annually from Alpha Epsilon Chapter of Delta Pi Epsilon at North Texas State University, Denton.

DOERS OF RESEARCH

First and foremost, doers of research are extensive users of research. They regularly read the journals and expend effort to be well informed about the research being advanced in business education and related fields. They constantly seek better ways of conducting research by examining new methodology and research designs.

Professional business teachers also recognize that effective teaching requires an understanding of the most recent teaching methodology. Research can help in this endeavor. Simply defined, research is a systematic attempt to answer questions by providing objective and defensible conclusions. Thus the ultimate goal of research is to provide an extensive body of knowledge about a behavior, so that any related statement can be made with nearly absolute certainty.

Admittedly, there are many approaches used to select a research problem. Business education research studies commonly are designed from a perspective of advancing knowledge by exploring or expanding theories, applying theories to practice, resolving conflicting or contradictory findings of previous research studies, correcting faulty methodology in previous research studies, resolving conflicting opinions, and studying actual practice.[3] Although these categories may suggest a problem needing study, other more concrete sources of ideas are available.

Sources of ideas for needed research. The first step in conducting research is to spend sufficient effort and time in determining what needs to be studied. This procedure demands serious attention; shortcuts at this stage may result in a project that is neither meaningful or helpful.

There is no shortage of educational problems that should be studied. The difficulty is more likely to be the selection of one problem from the many that are available. However, the first step is to identify a research topic, and to be certain the problem chosen is appropriate and worthy of study. A good place to begin is by reviewing published suggestions.

COMPILATIONS OF RESEARCH IDEAS. Several sources are available that identify critical educational problems that should be studied by business educators. In 1988, Delta Pi Epsilon published the fourth edition of *Needed Research in Business Education* to provide ideas to researchers. This publication is a compilation of problem statements needing investigation as suggested by researchers in the field. The statements are categorized and presented in two ways: (1) 26 generic research questions applicable to multiple business education areas, so that researchers can define and apply them to the subject or general area of their interest and expertise; and (2) 115 research questions for specific business education subjects or areas. The publication is available for purchase from Delta Pi Epsilon, P.O. 4340, Little Rock, AR 72214.

Another guide for future vocational education research efforts is supplied in a 1987 study by Schmidt, Lynch, and Hall. This study identified the priorities for vocational education research and was completed as a part of

---

[3]Cates, Ward M. *A Practical Guide to Educational Research.* Englewood Cliffs, NJ: Prentice-Hall, 1985.

a Planning Grant for the National Center for Research in Vocational Education.[4] The primary objective of the study was to determine future vocational education research and development priorities based on input from current major providers of vocational education research and development. Twenty-eight organizations participated in the study, generating 122 statements of needed research in vocational education. The respondents were asked to then evaluate the 122 statements and place them in order of priority listing each statement's importance for future study. The statements were examined, classified, and reported by topical areas.

The eight topics with highest priority as determined in this study were:

1. Effectiveness (or evaluation) of vocational education
2. Vocational program development and improvement, including curriculum development
3. Basic skills development in vocational education
4. Policy studies in vocational education, including the impact of future workplace and societal changes in vocational education
5. Collaborative relationship development in vocational education
6. Vocational personnel development
7. Providing for students with special needs, including addressing issues of access and equity
8. Clarifying the role of vocational education and the federal role in vocational education.

A complete listing of the 122 research questions can be accessed through the Educational Resources Information Center (ERIC # ED293981, Priorities for Research and Development in Vocational Education).

OTHER RESEARCH AS A SOURCE. Researchers often discover research topics by reviewing scholarly research done by others in the field of business education or in related fields such as psychology, sociology, and philosophy. For example, dissertations generally include a list of additional research related to the study that merits further investigation. These "building-block" ideas can be useful for identifying and refining a research topic or problem.

PERSONAL BELIEFS. Some problems that need investigation emerge from personal experiences and beliefs. Perhaps there is a need to find an answer to a particular question that the teacher has faced in the classroom. For example, a teacher may be concerned about which method is more effective in teaching students the basic skill of how to construct a paragraph. One method may appear to be more effective to the teacher, but a more critical evaluation demands that such a hypothesis be tested systematically.

TRICKLE-DOWN APPROACH. Another effective method of selecting a problem for research begins with a list of broad research categories such as evaluation. Such a topic is far too broad and must be narrowed in focus before it should be considered for a research project. The researcher should reflect on how this general topic of evaluation might be divided. Some reasonable sub-

[4]Schmidt, B. June; Lynch, Richard L.; and Hall, Shirley L. *Priorities for Research and Development in Vocational Education.* Research conducted as a part of a Planning Grant for the National Center for Research in Vocational Education, 1987.

categories might be evaluation of curriculum, evaluation of personnel, evaluation of students, evaluation of teaching methods, and evaluation of teaching materials and equipment.

Next, the researcher should select one of these subcategories for further refinement. If evaluation of teaching methods is a concern, make a list of recognized teaching methods. After reviewing the literature, narrow the topic to an investigation of only two methods—possibly the lecture method and the case method. Then decide how to proceed; perhaps the effectiveness of these two methods will be best evaluated by restricting the study to a particular course or class or a specified unit within a class.

This "trickle-down" approach for determining a research problem is based on dividing large topics into smaller units that will be manageable and that will provide findings that answer the research question. The selection of a topic that is too broad will usually result in research that tends to be "an inch thick and a mile wide" and does not adequately provide the answers sought.

Developing the framework. In choosing a problem to study, consideration must be given to the interests, skills, and situation of the researcher. Cates poses six questions that should form the framework for selecting a research problem for study.

1. Is the problem of interest to the researcher? Long hours are spent in working on studies, and if the problem is of little interest, motivation will lag.

2. Does the researcher have the necessary resources, especially time and money, to complete the study? Little will be gained by "putting off" a realistic assessment of the resources needed to complete a study and then matching that assessment with the availability of resources. This evaluation should be completed at the time a study topic is selected, so that if required resources are not available, the scope of the problem can be narrowed or an alternative study that needs fewer resources can be pursued.

3. Does the researcher possess the ability, knowledge, and training to carry on the study? Some researchers are competent in undertaking all facets of an investigation, while others may need help. For example, realizing that completing a study will require the availability of someone with technical expertise in computers or statistics can alert researchers to find such an individual, or the absence of required expertise indicates that such a study is beyond the researchers' capabilities. Sometimes such limitations can be overcome by consulting with knowledgeable research mentors and referring to textbooks addressing educational research.

4. Does the study make a contribution to education in general? Some research will produce findings generalizeable to a larger educational scope; however, some worthy research will apply only to a smaller locale, perhaps the business teacher's own classroom. A test is to decide whether the findings will produce useable answers to the questions under consideration. Could the scope of the study be broadened to provide answers to an expanded population with the available resources? If so, this opportunity should not be missed.

5. Is the research problem actually researchable? A researchable problem

requires that appropriate data is available for collection and analysis; otherwise, it is not a researchable problem.

6. Is the research problem trivial or overworked? In preparing a rationale for conducting a study, novice researchers are prone to rely on a statement such as "it has never been done." Sometimes the reason that the problem has never been studied is that it probably doesn't need to be. Such a study, at best, will yield data with little meaning, or the study will address a problem that has obvious findings.[5]

Common pitfalls. In order to function effectively in the classroom, a teacher does not need to study every variable known to exist that might have an effect on a behavior. Instead, the teacher needs only to be aware and knowledgeable about those variables deemed most important. A review of the related literature will provide an indication of those problems that have been investigated frequently over time. Unless new dimensions of the topic have arisen, avoid the selection of these overworked problems.

A pitfall to be avoided in selecting a problem to study is allowing the methodology or availability of a sample population to drive the study. Only after a problem is well defined and structured can the most appropriate way to conduct the investigation be planned.

Practicality, however, does dictate that the availability of observations must be a major concern of any researcher. An excellent study might be designed only to find that an appropriate sample is not available or is uncooperative. The result is that the study as designed cannot be completed; and the selection of an alternate population will yield findings that are questionable, possibly unreliable, and perhaps not even needed. For example, a research question might be formulated to determine the most effective way for teaching proofreading of typewritten documents to students enrolled in the inner-city Chicago high schools. The decision is made to conduct an experimental study with the students in several keyboarding classes located throughout the city. Although a convincing rationale might be developed that such a study is needed and would yield useful information, it would not be possible to conduct the experiment due to a policy adopted by the Chicago School Board that prohibits such research. This is the reason that research studies exclude Chicago and focus on the suburban schools or schools located elsewhere. However, conducting the study with students from the Chicago suburbs as the sample population will not produce a valid answer to the question asked.

Unfortunately, researchers often experience difficulty in gaining access to needed mailing lists; employers or employees from business, governmental, and educational organizations; and other persons who would comprise the appropriate sample. Even when access is achieved, those persons in the sample must be willing to participate. Researchers usually try to obtain a personal commitment from the sample population by interesting them in trying to solve the problem.

To insure that no harm will result from being a member of a population that is being studied, educational institutions usually require that a researcher

---

[5]Cates, *op. cit.*

complete a human subjects release form when conducting a research project in which students are involved. A university committee then approves or rejects the application based on legal ramifications.

Another factor that may have an influence on the selection of a research project involves the requirements of a Request for Proposal (RFP). These are formal requests issued by an organization or governmental agency requesting that researchers propose a study in which the problem is succinctly stated, the methodology is explained, the time frame required for completion is suggested, a budget is attached, and data sheets describing the credentials of the researcher are provided.

Many RFP's are rather rigid concerning the parameters of a research project that the organization will consider funding. This is because they are looking for capable persons to find answers through research to the specific questions they have. If the description of a research proposal fits the requirements, funding may be available; however, sometimes only certain types of expenses will be reimbursed. A thorough knowledge and understanding of the requirements is imperative.

Importance of question formulation. Care must be taken in writing the problem statement, since it must describe precisely what is to be achieved in the study. This is an important step in conducting research, and it is often the outgrowth of reviewing the literature and applying reflective thinking about the topic.

After a research question has been selected, the researcher needs to continue to review any related research that has been done. This review should be in greater depth and more focused than the initial review of the literature made when selecting a problem for study. The reasons for conducting this library research are (1) to become more knowledgeable about the subject; (2) to determine if the research question adequately explains what is being sought; and (3) to ascertain the extent to which the question has already been answered by others.

Only after a carefully defined research question is posed should consideration be given to the research design, because it is the research question that drives the methodology. A weakness of some studies is the appearance that the researcher is biased toward one methodology and tries, usually unsuccessfully, to adapt all research question to that methodology. The research method to be used depends on the research question under study.

Also, a design that uses a highly sophisticated and intricate statistical method of analysing the data may be far too unwieldy, and it may not contribute very much to solving the research problem. A more practical approach is to relate the method and extent of analysis to the use of the findings. Analysis is a tool to be used; it is not the essence of the research.

Design and methodology. In the four research studies discussed below, the problem dictates the design and methodology that needs to be followed in order to yield the desired results.

A recent award-winning study investigated the personal characteristics of women who have achieved upward mobility in information processing. A mail survey was sent to 625 female recipients of *Today's Office* in which the participants completed a questionnaire consisting of a Personal Data and Job History Form, Attitudes Toward Women Scale, and Personal Attributes Questionnaire.[6]

Although surveys can be an ineffectual method for gathering data for reasons of improper formulation of questions, improper sampling, inadequate returns, and the failure to select respondents who are capable and willing to cooperate, a survey was an appropriate method of gathering data for this study. Use of a questionnaire is an effective way to gather factual data, to survey feelings about situations, and to obtain measures of attitudes when personal interviews are impossible because of numbers or distance. The choice of the statistical tests was dependent upon the research problem under investigation.

An experimental research design elicits data of an entirely different kind since it involves identifying the relationship between two or more variables. For example, a 1988 study compared two methods for teaching word processing: one was a computer-based tutorial and the other a textbook-based approach for teaching use of word processing software at the collegiate level. Two instructors each taught an experimental and control section of word processing classes. Both cognitive and performance word processing achievement testing revealed that the two methods did not differ in their effectiveness.[7]

A study in the same content area that required a different design used meta-analysis to describe the effects of using word processing equipment in writing instruction. This problem had been studied by other researchers with a wide variety of conclusions. This method allows unbiased analysis and synthesis of already-completed research studies by statistically measuring and comparing the numerical data from these studies. Fourteen completed studies were found that addressed the problem of this dissertation. Meta-analysis formulas were applied and more comprehensive conclusions could be reached reflecting the previous research work.[8]

An example of qualitative research is a study on the use of vocational education courses to meet high school graduation requirements. Interviews and visits with school administrators were used to determine the factors which facilitated this categorization of vocational education courses. Since these factors could not be anticipated beforehand, on-site visits and involvement with schools were necessary to discern the contributing circumstances for recognizing vocational preparation as meeting high school graduation requirements.[9]

Collaborative research efforts. There are several advantages to teachers working together on a research study. First, such an arrangement will allow for interdisciplinary thinking that can result from combining the efforts,

[6]Davidson, E. J. *Women in Information Processing Careers: Sex-Role Identity, Attitudes Towards Women,* and *Other Selected Variables.* Doctor's thesis. New York: New York University, 1987.

[7]Orr, C. *A Comparison of Achievement and Attitudes of Post-Secondary Students Taught by Two Methods of Instruction in Word Processing.* Doctor's thesis. St. Paul: University of Minnesota, 1988.

[8]Schram, Robert M. *The Effects of Using Word Processing Equipment in Writing Instruction: A Meta-Analysis.* Doctor's thesis. DeKalb: Northern Illinois University, 1989.

[9]Copa, G. *Vocational Education and High School Graduation Requirements.* St. Paul: University of Minnesota, Minnesota Research and Development Center for Vocational Education, 1989.

knowledge, and background of teachers from more than one discipline. Such interaction will tend to broaden business teachers' perspective and provide an opportunity to investigate problems with wider appeal. Critics frequently cite a lack of interdisciplinary thinking of faculty as an inherent weakness of the present-day educational system.

Collaborative efforts provide a welcome opportunity for business teachers to inform teachers from other disciplines about problems and issues in business education. An observation often voiced is that business educators talk too much to others within their field and too little to teachers in other areas. If an interdisciplinary approach does not appear to be feasible, a team approach that combines the skills, knowledge, and expertise of faculty members from a business education department may be successfully utilized.

National research studies sponsored by professional organizations may allow for research of a wider magnitude than could otherwise be contemplated. A national study sponsored by Delta Pi Epsilon in 1989 was designed to determine the status of typewriting/keyboarding in elementary schools and needed input from many teachers from across the nation.[10] The cooperation of teachers willing to assist contributes greatly to the success of such projects. This expanded participation often stimulates researchers to pursue the study of more complex problems,

Researchers often find it necessary to ask several business teachers for assistance, such as completing a survey instrument, interviewing selected persons from a population sample, or administering a test to students in classes. Other requests might include serving as a member of a pilot study to review a questionnaire for clarity and understanding or evaluate a research design being proposed. The willingness of business teachers to assist researchers in the quest for knowledge is a professional contribution greatly appreciated and has a potential to result in the development of greater teacher expertise in business classrooms at the secondary and postsecondary levels.

Sources of funding. Business teachers who need financial assistance for their research should be aware of sources that provide funding on a regular basis. Sources that specifically encourage research in business education through funding include:

Delta Pi Epsilon Research Foundation
Mankato State University, Mankato, MN 56001
(A specified proposal is required; inquiries should be sent to the national headquarters. The Foundation is interested in funding individual or corraborative research in business education. No funding is available for dissertations.)

National Business Education Association (NBEA)
1914 Association Drive, Reston, VA 22091
NBEA is in the process of initiating a scholarship program for business educators. The scholarship may be used for graduate work or to conduct research.)

Office Systems Research Association (OSRA)
College of Business Administration, Western Kentucky University

---

[10]Sormunen, Carolee and others. *A National Study of Instructional Practices and Perceptions of Elementary School Teachers About Typewriting/Keyboarding.* Little Rock, AR: Delta Pi Epsilon, 1989.

501 Guse Hall, Bowling Green, KY 42101
(Office systems research is supported through minigrants; funding serves as seed money to assist with initial research costs. Proposals for minigrants are encouraged from graduate students, faculty, and business professionals.)

Many other professional organizations offer research grants for which business educators are eligible. Generally, the only requirement is that the researcher be a member of the organization. *Phi Delta Kappa* has funds available for educational research projects; the average grant is in the $750 to $1,000 range. For additional information, contact Phi Delta Kappa, P.O. Box 789, Bloomington, IN 47402-0789.

Many universities have instituted an office that will provide information on sources of funding for research projects. They usually keep current guidelines on file and any information concerning application deadlines for proposal submission.

SUMMARY

The use of research as a means for improving business education programs requires the full participation of all members of the profession. While not all will be *doers* of research, all should be *users* of research carried out by others. Those who benefit from others' research efforts can also play an essential role by cooperating in the refinement of research testing instruments and data collection efforts. Thoughtful completion of questionnaires is a small act, but it has an important effect on the quality of research findings.

Both the doers and users of research play an important role in maintaining the quality and availability of a literature base for the field. The dissemination of research in respected journals is important to the visibility and legitimacy of the field. Researchers support these journals by submitting their manuscripts for publication consideration; they benefit professionally from publication of their work in respected, refereed journals. The users of business education research, likewise, benefit from having access to this literature. Subscriptions to these journals and professional membership in their sponsoring organizations are the necessary votes of confidence from business educators that help maintain the research vitality of the field.

CHAPTER 12

Exercising Political Savvy: A Routine Workout For Every Educator

RUTH E. BROOKS

J. Everett Light Career Center, Indianapolis, Indiana

ROBERT J. THOMPSON

Foothill College (Retired), Los Altos Hills, California

Knowledgeable professional business educators, alert to the dynamics of policy making, have always known that education in a free society which involves parliamentary mechanisms for resource allocation cannot be isolated from political decision making. These educators, with support from organizations such as NBEA and AVA, have been assertive in making sure that education is allotted its share of resources and have utilized the political process to do so. Business educators can learn lessons in political astuteness from the early history of vocational education as it attempted to reform the public schools through federal legislation. The lesson to be learned is that exercising political savvy must be a routine workout for every business educator. The steps in the workout parallel the steps that an athlete takes to prepare to win.

MIND SET AND COMMITMENT

Before an athlete even begins to work out, a mind set and commitment to goals must be established. Three elements comprise this focus: advocacy, historical perspective, and impact of the goal.

Advocacy. Advocacy is a term that carries with it a commitment to the belief that the issue is of value not only to yourself and your constituency, but to the public as well. For educational issues this means that the issue is good for the students as well as for the teaching profession. Teachers have a strong commitment to their profession and membership in the National Business Education Association is one step in the direction of advocacy.

For many years in educational circles, the word "politics" created an element of discomfort or unease. Here we are after nearly a century of public policy enactments regarding education and there are many people who would like to believe that education is isolated from politics.

Bailey and his associates point out that educational decision making is invariably a political exercise:

> More public money is spent for education than for any other single function of state and local government . . . . All over the United States school boards are elected

131

or appointed through a highly political process . . . . The size, location, cost, looks, and facilities of school buildings are frequently matters of high political controversy . . . . In short, education is one of the most thoroughly political enterprises in American life—or for that matter in the life of any society.[1]

Rosenthal has provided definitions of politics and power as they relate to education. Politics refers to the methods by which social values and resources are allocated for different purposes and among different people. Power, tied closely to politics, is the relative ascendancy or predominance of one individual or group over others, with regard to particular values, resources, or objectives. If political processes allocate values and resources, then the distribution and exercise of power determine who gets what, when, and how.[2]

The impact of reform movements in education is one way in which political decision making in education may be viewed. The variables of the impact of reform are wide-ranging, but certain key characteristics are identifiable in any full-fledged reform movement. These are: (a) nature of the leadership, (b) nature and method of criticism of existing system, (c) objectives of reform or proposals for change, (d) method of articulation or influence, (e) method of aggregation or consolidation of opposing views, (f) controversies, tensions, and difficult issues to resolve, and (g) nature of impact.

Historical perspective on the importance of and attitudes about business/ vocational education. Even though analyses of politics, power, and educational decision making have only been visible in recent times, the early leaders of vocational education could have written the texts on these very topics. The work of Charles A. Prosser and his contemporaries could serve as a classic primer in educational politics and decision making. They led a reform movement designed to change an educational system; their efforts have been called the most successful of school reform movements in the history of education in America. Edson spells out why it has been so successful:

> I address my remarks to a particular educational reform—vocational education— one that in my view was, and continues to be, a "successful" reform. By successful, I mean that as a result of a reform effort, changes took place that have become permanently imbedded in both the structure and ideology of American public schooling. These changes may be understood in terms of structural innovations (such as the comprehensive high school, the junior high school, and vocational guidance), in the creation of new groups with vested interests in maintaining those structures (such as vocational teacher education teachers, guidance counselors, and IQ testers), and perhaps most importantly, in terms of an emerging ideological consensus that schools can—and should—prepare youth for jobs.[3]

Business educators need to identify all the variables that have related to their stability in education above and beyond those success factors that Edson mentioned. How much difference has involvement with employer advisory

[1] Bailey, S.K., and others. *Schoolmen and Politics: A Study of State Aid to Education in the Northeast.* Syracuse, NY: Syracuse University Press, 1962.

[2] Rosenthal, A. *Governing Education: A Reader on Politics, Power, and Public School Policy.* Garden City, NY: Anchor Books, Doubleday and Co., 1969.

[3] Edson, C.J. "The Reform of Vocational Education: The Relationship Between Jobs and Schooling." *Urban Education* 12:451; 1978.

groups made? How have the model curriculum standards and guidelines in some states been a factor? To what extent has the issue of work experience education programs in conjunction with classroom instruction been a factor? Research on these political aspects has not been completed.

Impact of the reform movement. Business education has strong support at the local and state levels throughout the country. By using advisory councils made up of employers, vocational education has won the support of local people. The fact that funding has become heavily weighted toward local and state contribution is an indication of this support. Particularly with the recent emphasis on providing a relevant education for the handicapped and the disadvantaged, vocational education has proven, at the local and state levels, its potential contribution to these clients. This reform movement has uniquely demonstrated that a general and common curriculum is not exclusive enough for the public school student. Structural and ideological changes have been made because of the movement.

The following conclusions are offered in relation to politics of vocational education:

1. The grass-roots approach is central to the previous success of business education; it must be preserved at all costs. New strategies should be designed to maintain this support.

2. Business education should not rely only on its practitioners for support. It should seek diverse group support. New groups should be identified that can see the value of business education to their cause.

3. If federal support is withdrawn from vocational education, the business educators should accelerate efforts to address design features of the vocational education delivery system in an effort to provide cohesiveness.

4. The political success of vocational education will rest a great deal on the knowledge the field is able to communicate. This knowledge base must be organized and interpreted in concise, but informative ways. Political strategies are ineffective if factual information is not available.

5. Strategies should be sought at all costs to strengthen and develop leadership for business education that can deal effectively with business and industry, labor, legislators, and educators.

As business educators look to the future, it becomes increasingly more apparent that they must become more adept in the politics of vocational education.

WARM UP: KNOWING THE PROCESS

After the mind set and commitment to prepare for a goal, a good warm up is the next step. A warm up for a political workout consists of knowing the impact of current legislation and being familiar with the changing economy and workplace.

Impact of current legislation. When Russia beat the United States in the space race during the early 1960's, it was immediately decided that *every* American student would receive an "academic" education. As a result, the needs of those who had no plans to attend college were ignored. Since our school systems at that time only met the educational needs of a few, the dropout rate increased drastically. Those students needing skills to survive in the business world were not prepared to meet the needs of employers. When the plight of America's students was recognized, the Vocational Education Act of 1963 became a reality. Although vocational (occupational) education has not been the total answer to education's problems, vocational programs have become an integral part of the comprehensive educational arena.

With the Vocational Education Act of 1963, money became available not only for existing vocational programs at the secondary and postsecondary levels but also for business education programs. Students who completed business education classes were now being prepared for the "world of work."

Federal policy, it seems, has been the driving force for vocational education in the United States; and the Carl D. Perkins Act has continued to substantiate that philosophy.[4] The purpose of the Carl D. Perkins Act is to provide education and educational opportunities for the largest segment of the American work force—high school students and graduates who have not attended or who will not attend college. This legislation provides guidelines for implementing this belief, but it delegates to the states much of the responsibility for deciding how policy should be implemented and how funds are to be allocated among school districts and postsecondary institutions.

States who have set vocational education priorities have realized that such programs do increase students' chances for job placement and success, do provide more productive employees, and do produce employees that require less formal on-the-job training than those employees without relevant training.

It is important, therefore, that the American voice be heard supporting the reauthorization of the Carl D. Perkins Act. Once again, priorities at the federal level will drive action at the state level.

The changing economy and workplace. During the next 20 years, technological advances, increasing international competition, and demographic changes will probably change our economy and our way of life more dramatically than at any other time in our history.

In light of this changing economy, the following issues will need to be addressed:

1. Economic growth will need to be stimulated.

2. Productivity will need to be improved.

3. The aging work force will need to be utilized.

4. Minorities will need to be more fully integrated into the work force.

5. Workers' education and skills will need to be improved.

6. Women's roles with work and families will need to be defined and accepted.

Work force 2000: Work and Workers for the Twenty-first Century, a study conducted by the Hudson Institute for the U.S. Department of Labor, states

---

[4]Weber, James M., and Puleo, Nancy F. *Dynamics of Secondary Programs Assisted Under the Carl D. Perkins Act.* Columbus: The National Center for Research in Vocational Education, The Ohio State University, 1988.

the following about the upcoming work force that will be dealing with the above issues.

1. The population and work force will grow more slowly than at any time since the 1930's. There will be fewer people, therefore, to produce needed goods and services.

2. The average age of the work force will rise. There will be more retirees and fewer young workers.

3. Women will make up almost two-thirds of those entering the work force.

4. Minorities will make up 29 percent of the new work force entrants, twice the current figure.

5. Immigrants will represent the largest share of the increase in population and work force since the first World War.

In addition, this study points out that the majority of jobs in the United States will require some kind of postsecondary education; 27 percent of the new jobs—compared to 40 percent today—will require low-skilled workers; and jobs currently considered to be in the middle of the skill requirement range will be the low-skilled occupations of the future.[5]

To meet these economical and work force changes, education must be responsive and futuristic. Tomorrow's students will need a far better education just to get a decent job, and this is because the growing employment areas are those that require training beyond a high school diploma. Schools will have to meet these new demands, and they will have to have the help of parents, community, and business.

STARTING LINE: GETTING THE FACTS

It is at the starting line that many races are won or lost. The starting line for a political objective is the process of getting the facts together. Two parts to fact gathering are important: identifying the pertinent issues and making the case.

Identifying issues pertinent to business/vocational education. William Christopher, Commissioner of the Indiana Commission on Vocational and Technical Education, said that when we look at education in this country we see that:

- 25 percent of students who enter high school don't complete it.
- 38 percent of high school graduates seek employment after high school.
- 50 percent of those who enter college do not graduate four years later.
- Job preparation is among the top ranked reasons why parents want their children to get an education.
- Traditional academic instruction motivates and appeals to only 20 percent of students.

Business educators: Now is the time to market business classes and prove that business education does address these concerns!

---

[5]*Workforce 2000: A Discussion Paper.* Washington, D.C.: U.S. Department of Education, 1988.

Business education, as well as other elective areas, has its own problems and concerns, however. What about declining enrollments, increased graduation requirements, changing technology, high dropout rates, at-risk students, inadequate funding, back-to-the-basic movement, and global economic awareness? There are basically four options for business educators —maintain, modernize, change the current programs, or die! Since education is legislated, the place to start is in your state. Now is the time to act!

Making the case. It is safe to say that today's education system cannot begin to totally prepare students for the world they will enter upon graduation from high school. Marvin J. Cetron, in his article "Class of 2000," says that about 10 years ago approximately 77 percent of jobs involved at least some time spent in generating, processing, retrieving, or distributing information.[6] By the year 2000, Cetron believes that figure will be 95 percent, and that nearly all information processing will be computerized. If these figures are even reasonably correct, one has to realize that business education skills will be needed and required for everyone's career.

Business education is a very large elective department in the public school system, and the mission of business education is to educate students *for* and *about* business. Therefore, business education is comprised of two components: (1) business and economic education for all students to develop economic literacy and consumer skills; and (2) occupational preparation for students planning to enter the work force immediately after graduation and for those needing employment skills necessary to finance postsecondary and collegiate education.

One of the most widely recognized educational values of business education is the frequent "real world" application of basic skills so important to all students today. High school accounting courses apply math and computer skills. Writing, computation, speaking, and nonverbal communications skills are used in a variety of classes including Business Communications, Business Math, and Introduction to Business. The opportunity to develop further critical-thinking and problem-solving skills is provided in courses like Business Law, Business Computer Applications, and Business Economics.

Business education offers students the chance to develop leadership, social, civic, and occupational skills through student organizations such as the Business Professionals of America and the Future Business Leaders of America. Through these organizations, students hold elected and appointed positions, participate in competitive events, and conduct projects for the benefit of the community.

Through articulation agreements, cooperative efforts are being implemented between secondary and postsecondary schools; and in the near future, students and teachers will be able to identify competencies and the level at which students will have the opportunity to achieve them.

Business education *does* prepare students for tomorrow's labor force as well as for higher education. It does, through its practical, hands-on application approach, respond to students' needs in basic skill reinforcement, entrepreneurial and business ownership, technology, and global economics.

[6]Cetron, Marvin J. "Class of 2000." *The Futurist,* November/December 1988.

136

ACTION

An action plan for any legislative activity on behalf of business education includes making annual plans to address educational issues and forming ongoing legislative committees and professional action committees.

Annual plans to address educational issues. Annual plans are necessary for consistency in direction. The annual plan of an association often takes the form of a Program of Work. In order for this plan to be effective, it must be reviewed on a regular basis and approved by the representative body of the organization.

The fundamental purpose of a plan is to define the unifying themes and directions for business education in the public schools. It should outline in clear terms the general mission of business education taught in all levels of the public education system. It is intended to inform national, state, and local policy makers, students, parents, employers, and general citizenry about the goals and directions of public education in addressing the most critical issues confronting it in preparation of youth and adults for their role as productive and satisfied members of the work force.

The National Business Education Association has a program of work that is agreed upon by the NBEA Executive Board. In addition, the Policies Commission for Business and Economic Education issues periodic Policy Statements. Planning a course of action requires an understanding of the conditions of the time in order that the plan will produce the outcome that can be uniformly subscribed to. The 1986 statement illustrates this direction:

> Criticism of public education in recent years has had a dramatic impact on the educational programs in the United States. The "back-to-basics" movement, reports from national and state commissions, and criticisms by media have caused society to take a serious look at educational institutions and their effectiveness in providing quality education. . . .
>
> Since legislators play a very significant role in educational funding and decision making and because certain legislation has had an adverse impact on business education, we believe that business educators must consider legislation and the legislative process a major concern to be addressed. . . .[7]

Ongoing legislative committees/professional action committees. NBEA has an ongoing legislative action committee composed of representatives from each of the regions and supplemented by members from various state associations. The national committee is responsible for establishing a network of regional and state committees that will carry out the program of work of the committee.

Communicating to the membership the legislative issues and information such as legislative reports and analysis at the national level is a key activity of the national committee. The committee members bring state and regional issues to the committee and in this way a representative voice in policy decisions is achieved.

---

[7]*Policies Commission for Business and Economic Education.* "This We Believe About the Role of Business Educators in Influencing Legislation." *Business Education Forum* 41:13; October 1986.

137

A strategy of the committee is to increase the business educators' involvement in the legislative process through an effective legislative network. The network starts with the NBEA Executive Board and the headquarters staff. It involves cooperative planning with the Business and Office Education Division of the American Vocational Association and a combined effort to unify a process to effect legislation.

The NBEA Executive Board develops and communicates the legislative policy and position statements. The NBEA headquarters office solicits, receives and analyzes information on legislative issues and concerns through the communications network and forwards these to the Board.

The NBEA Legislative Committee communicates information about legislative issues affecting business education to the legislative network. Appropriate strategies are reviewed and suggestions for action are distributed.

The five NBEA regions are kept informed on legislative issues and activities in Congress. The regions maintain communication with the state associations and keep the chain of the network in place.

The state associations make up the action group. It is at this grass roots level that all working legislative committees find success or failure. A working legislative committee within each of the congressional districts is an essential. Key individuals must be identified for this legislative activity. They must initiate activities within the district to maintain a close working relationship with congressional and state legislators. They can inform the legislator of the Association's priorities and positions on specific issues. The feedback from the members of Congress regarding their positions on relevant issues must be reported to the regional and national committee. Strategies can be developed to assist in the passing of policy issues as a result of feedback.

Members must be kept informed concerning legislative issues. This network serves as a communication and action vehicle on legislation that affects business education. Individual members must be alert to the issues and provided with the skills to communicate with the member of their congressional district.

HOME STRETCH

As in any race, much can happen in the home stretch to win or lose a position. Some of the elements that can ensure success are use of specific strategies to influence legislation, communicating with a legislator in proven ways, and utilizing a set of guidelines for network contacts.

Specific strategies to influence legislation. The federal legislative process is lengthy and complex, but it is one of the bulwarks of our representative system of government and deserves support. One of the most practical safeguards of the American democratic way of life, the legislative process gives ample opportunity to all sides to be heard and make their views known. The fact that a proposal cannot become law without consideration and approval by both houses of Congress is an outstanding virtue of the congressional system. Open and full discussions, provided for under the Constitution, frequently result in either the notable improvement of a bill by amendment before it becomes law or the complete defeat of a bad proposal.

With the great variety and number of bills introduced in today's legislative sessions, no single legislator can possibly understand every issue and bill. Legislators have come to depend on outside sources to interpret legislation for them. Information from members of organizations often provides the foundation for new legislation or for the amending of existing programs.

Most of what state associations do is not considered lobbying. An association may legally provide information to legislators. There are very strict lobbying laws in most states, but these laws usually do not include activities by individuals with their own legislators. Lobbying laws usually do govern activities with legislators other than your own.

The role of an association person is to explain, inform, and persuade—not to attack, threaten, or belittle. The elected officials are to be referred to and treated with courtesy and respect, regardless of positions taken. Courteous persistence can wear down resistance. Visits and contacts should be short and meaningful.

How to communicate with your legislator. As the person who votes for a legislator, you are the one responsible for providing input to the congressional office through correspondence, a personal visit, or conducting a group meeting. At the beginning of each legislative session, both the Senate and House publish lists of committees and their members. You will need these lists to find out who is on the committee handling legislation that concerns you. Because a bill may go through many revisions before being reported out of committee, your legislator rarely pays attention to it until it is reported out unless, of course, it arises in his or her own committee. Knowing when to write is important. It is best to write to the legislator who represents your own district. In communicating with elected representatives never use form or copied letters. Even if your legislator is not on the committee concerned with your particular problem, you should contact the office directly to make the personal committee contact.

Remember that Congress always convenes in January and begins committee hearings as soon as possible. Exact timing on reports, floor action, and conferences depends on the amount of controversy surrounding a legislative proposal and the priority placed on it by the President and congressional leadership.

Legislative network contact guidelines. You have agreed to assist in the legislative effort for business education in your state. As a network contact you will be assisting in obtaining the support of specific legislators at the federal and state levels. The key to this program is identifying constituents of each legislator who can get to know the legislator and staff. You will be asked to assist in getting key support on legislation from time to time.

Your duties include:

1. GETTING TO KNOW LEGISLATOR AND STAFF. Every attempt has been made to assign only one business educator to each legislator. You should get to know that legislator and staff—both at the district office and in the capital city. You should find out the names and phone numbers of key staff members

in the legislator's organization, and the philosophy and position of the legislator regarding education, particularly vocational education. Also, get information about the committees on which that legislator serves. Then arrange to meet with the legislator to discuss vocational education in the district. Know what is happening in other programs within the district.

2. ARRANGING FOR VISITS TO BUSINESS EDUCATION PROGRAMS. On a regular basis, get the legislator to visit a specific business education program in action.

3. SERVING AS A LEGISLATIVE CONTACT. From time to time you will be asked to communicate with your legislator regarding a specific piece of legislation. You should be familiar with the legislation before the contact. Be sure that you give the position on the bill established by the state legislative committee. If the legislator asks for opinions on a specific piece of legislation check your answer out with the legislative committee.

4. SHARING THE LEGISLATIVE POLICY STATEMENT. The state legislative committee may establish a legislative position paper or policy. You may be asked to communicate this policy statement to the legislator and to defend it. You should be prepared to do so and should check with the committee when you have questions about the policy.

5. PRESENTING LEGISLATION. The state might decide to carry a specific piece of legislation through a legislator whom you know. The legislative committee would prepare the legislation and present the case. Your role would be to convince the legislator to defend the legislation (or introduce the bill).

6. BECOMING INVOLVED IN THE POLITICAL PROCESS. You should review the legislative process and relevant time lines. Many legislators say that they listen most to those who have been active supporters. Don't be afraid to get involved in campaigns and support specific legislators who have been supportive of vocational education.

You should be able to share other hints as to the best ways to carry out the duties of an active network contact with other members of the committee. Your assistance can make a difference in the support of business education in the state and nation.

COOL DOWN

After a race, whether successful at winning or placing, a cool down helps the athlete build on the experience of the race and allows him to recover to participate in another race at another time. The following information is contained in a statement issued by the Policies Commission for Business and Economic Education in 1986 on the role of business education in influencing legislation:

Business Education Professional Associations
We believe that national, state, and local business education professional associations must take a pro-active stance regarding legislation. They must pursue an aggressive legislative plan of action to deal with issues that affect business education, and they must coordinate the efforts and actions of their members. The legislative plan should include the following:

• Strategies for aggressive action to support or reject proposals that affect business education

- Annual plans of action to address identified legislative issues
- Ongoing legislative committees to develop the association's positions, strategies, and plans of action on all legislative matters
- Networks to provide communication on legislative matters and to elicit appropriate unified action.

To accomplish the legislative plans most effectively, **we believe that** professional business education associations should contract with business education advocates to (1) keep members up to date on the events taking place in the fast-moving legislative arena; (2) advise the associations and their members on legislative matters; and (3) promote business education to business, legislators, and state and federal education agencies.

We believe that business education professional associations must take a leadership role in bringing together associations representing other educational groups to present a unified front to legislators on matters of mutual concern. Consequently, business educators must establish procedures for communication with these groups so that we all may speak with one voice and become a great force in influencing legislation.

We believe that business education professional associations should initiate and support legislation that provides adequate funding for curriculum development, faculty development, instructional equipment and supplies, and research projects.

We believe that business education professional associations as well as members must involve the business community in obtaining support in legislative matters.

State Level Business Education Personnel

We believe that business education representatives from agencies such as state departments of education should become actively involved in providing information to business educators concerning legislative matters. One way of accomplishing this involvement is to have business education representatives from agencies serve on boards and committees of state business education professional associations.

Business Educators

Since legislators are more sensitive to the needs of their own constituents, **we believe that** business educators must become actively involved at the local level in developing positive relationships with their legislators. These relationships should provide opportunities to—

- Explain the goals and purposes of business education
- Enumerate the benefits of business education to the students and to the community
- Cite the contributions of business education to the economy
- Describe the needs of business education and suggest ways of meeting them
- Seek support on legislative issues
- Influence educational policy.

We believe that business educators must work closely with business personnel to convince them of the importance of business education programs and the support needed from the community. In addition, they should involve business personnel as advocates for legislative action to improve the effectiveness of the business education program.

Education IS legislated! Therefore, business educators must become actively involved in the legislative process to affect actions that lead to the improvement of business education.[8]

---

[8]*Ibid.*

CHAPTER 13

Interning, Co-oping, and Programming Alternatives: Successful Partnerships and Funding

JOYCE CATON

Hazelwood School District, Florissant, Missouri

CONNIE BUCK

Louisiana State Department of Education, Baton Rouge

The challenge of the 1990's continues to be searching for new ways to deal with social, educational, and economic needs of a diverse population. Statistics about dropouts—as many as one million each year—are staggering to a nation that prides itself on education. Statistics related to the labor force—75 percent of new entrants to the labor force in the next 15 years will be women and other minorities—stress urgency in the need for flexible training programs. Statistics about changing employment opportunities— different skills and obsolete jobs—indicate major revisions in instructional delivery methods. Global involvement both in economic competition abroad and cultural infiltration at home are other reasons that make educational reform crucial.

Few, if any, argue that all of these reasons and more make the educational arena a challenging one. No one argues that programs must be flexible and current. Most agree that educational opportunities can be provided in places outside the traditional classroom environment. More and more people are realizing that working relationships and joint ventures with forces outside the traditional classroom environment must be coordinated and bidirectional benefits must be afforded.

Business education has not been stagnant in developing and implementing alternative programs in attempting to meet the diverse needs of unique populations and the tedious demands of technology. Internships, cooperative programs, and other innovative educational alternatives can provide occupational experiences and training that better meet the diverse needs of students and teachers. They also can utilize most effectively the available resources of educational and business entities.

INTERNING

Technology used in the classroom is frequently behind industry due to financial restraints and the nature or lack of ability of educational systems to change rapidly. Additionally, classroom teachers are often removed from the office environment and have a difficult time staying abreast of changes in the business environment.

Intern programs afford clients the opportunities of first-hand observation and involvement in the most modern aspects of a field. Generally, an intern program offers observation for advanced students in a professional field. Intern programs can go beyond the regular classroom in offering an array of activities in a short period of time. Interning can provide movement throughout an organizational structure so that one can get to know more about the goals and activities of the entire organization.

Manpower, Inc., and the National Business Education Association have attempted to develop a business intern program that will allow business educators to view and work with the new technology that can not be found in most classrooms. Implemented in 1987, this "Bridging the Gap" program provides teachers the chance to move from the classroom to a working environment through temporary work assignments. Participating teachers go through the same procedures as other Manpower applicants. There is a regular interview, skills assessment, identification of particular strengths and weaknesses, and access to specialized computer training. Working short terms in a variety of business-related jobs allows an educator to view and use the most up-to-date equipment. Additionally, teachers learn what materials and methods need to be updated and what students will be required to know to meet the expectations of the business world. Teachers can use their on-the-job experiences to modernize their curriculum and teaching strategies.

Past participants in the "Bridging the Gap" program have made these observations:

- The use of modern equipment in the work force has created a greater need for self-taught training techniques. Following oral and written instructions from manuals or videotapes is critical.
- The need for self-directed workers is essential.
- Communication skills and basic skills remain the number one requirement for all workers.
- The ability to accept and adapt to change is difficult but very necessary.
- Skills are important, but students must also understand why skills are important.
- Analytical skills must be developed.

The intern program established between NBEA and Manpower also goes beyond what the business educator can observe or learn from an on-the-job experience. The focus of any business program has to be its relevancy to the business world. The NBEA-Manpower program provides a mechanism where business teachers can increase their awareness of the changing business environment while developing a linkage with business and industry. Such a linkage can create a strong partnership that highlights the viability of the business education program as an essential and integral component of a school system. (For more information on "Bridging the Gap," contact Laurie Anderson, Information Coordinator, Manpower, Inc., P.O. Box 2053, Milwaukee, WI 53201.)

Students can also benefit from intern programs. These programs vary in design but are common in purpose. Students can earn credit toward graduation or toward the completion of specific high school courses. Intern programs may include working with several agencies over a period of time or with one business or company. A student interning in the insurance field could observe and work with an individual agent and progress to a regional office. A student could be assigned to intern at a travel agency for a period of time and then be rotated to a specific transportation area such as an airline or bus company. Such a rotation would provide a strong overview of the career. Generally, a teacher or counselor is assigned the task of placing students in intern assignments that relate to a specific course or a career interest. For example, a student may be placed at a local stock brokerage firm and earn credit for economics; or a student could serve as an aide to a lawyer to earn credit in business law. The program leader is responsible for developing a plan or study and overseeing the student's experiences. Care must be taken to insure that the internship affords the student a variety of experiences related to the curriculum and a clear insight into the specific career area. Preplanning and collaboration among all concerned is essential. Intern programs depend on community involvement, administrative support, and a creative leader.

COOPERATIVE PROGRAMS

Work experience has been advocated for several years as a culminating activity in a student's preparation for employment. Cooperative education is such a program designed to focus on student, work, and a partnership with an entity outside the structured school environment. Cooperative education as an umbrella term is often used to describe several varied educational opportunities. Such programs involve "real work" experience of some nature and encompass such areas as on-the-job training, occupational experiences, work experience, work study, and cooperative programs. While the ultimate purpose is to allow a student to gain insight into an actual job, the approaches, objectives and outcomes vary widely.

On-the-job training. On the job training implies task-related instruction. Instruction is "learning by doing" in an actual or simulated situation. On-the-job training for a student can be exploratory or occupational and may be accomplished in a variety of settings. Exploratory on-the-job training helps students identify job traits in relation to their abilities and characteristics. Students generally observe various work sites and spend several hours shadowing individual workers in a number of different occupations. Such experiences may be extremely appropriate for junior or middle high school students or for students considered to be "at-risk." Simulated situations also can provide a type of on-the-job training. Most major publishing companies have developed simulations that cover a multiple of abilities and tasks. There are also simulation opportunities that have been developed for computer use.

Occupational experience. Occupational experience refers to on-the-job activities which are related to specific occupational areas being studied or for which study has been completed in school. Students work during or after regular school hours and/or during summer months. Extra credit toward graduation may be given for this work. The teacher may find suitable workstations for students, may provide individualized instruction, and usually supervises students at work. Students may work in self- or family-owned or managed enterprises or for other employers.

General work experience. Students are provided opportunities to experience employment or volunteer work structured to develop an understanding and appreciation of factors that lead to successful careers. Work experience students obtain employment in jobs not requiring prior knowledge or training. Many educational disciplines may have general work experience for cultural enrichment, community service, or career awareness.

Vocational teachers can be helpful in the placement of students, and a project director or teacher can oversee activities. Students may be released from school part of the day or may work after school hours, on weekends, and during vacation periods. Students may also be given school credit.

Work study. Various legislative acts have provided reimbursement funds to educational entities for compensation of students who are employed by public agencies. Such work and compensation are provided to make it financially feasible for students to remain in school and complete an occupational preparation program. Employment provided for work study students may not necessarily be related to occupational objectives, but it does provide a means for helping these students develop attitudes and practices essential to continued successful employment. Work study programs are administered and supervised by project directors who are responsible for locating and placing the students in jobs and seeing that all regulations governing the work study project are followed. Work study programs are often available through state or local legislative acts. Federal provisions through the Carl Perkins Act or the Job Training Partnership Act have been common sources for such programs.

Cooperative education. Cooperative education refers to a teaching method in an occupational preparation program of vocational education whereby students alternate their school schedule between in-school and on-the-job learning activities. Students attend school and take required academic subjects as well as a class related to their occupational preparation program. Students are provided release time for on-the-job instruction in the occupational area of their career choice.

A professionally trained teacher-coordinator teaches the students in school, locates suitable workstations, and supervises their work education. The coordinator develops with the employer, parents, and student a training plan that includes an instructional plan for the student and assures that the classroom and on-the-job activities are merged into a single occupational preparation program. Students receive credit toward graduation for the combination of school and on-the-job instruction and are paid for the wage-producing activities of the job.

A growing movement over the past few years has been the development of cooperative work experience programs at the postsecondary level. These programs are designed to employ undergraduate students in industry, business, and government organizations for specific periods of time. Employment positions usually are related to their major field of study or career choice. Cooperative education is a blend of theory and practice and bridges the gap between the student, the employer, and the university. Many postsecondary programs are designed to provide students with increasing responsibilities commensurate with their academic skills and experience. Students work in "parallel" or "alternating" arrangements. Parallel arrangements permit the student to attend school while working part-time. Alternate arrangements allow the student a period (semester or quarter) of full-time work followed by a period of full-time study.

PROGRAMMING ALTERNATIVES

Business educators have traditionally looked upon cooperative work experience models as a delivery system for students to receive training beyond the walls of the classroom for entry-level employment. In recent years this delivery system has failed to attract the number of students it once did for a variety of reasons. Students lack time in their schedules for elective courses as a result of increased graduation requirements. Students with a career goal that requires postsecondary education may lack interest in cooperative work experience programs due to the sometimes limited scope of the experiences in the typical cooperative workstation. Consequently, this important link between the classroom and the world of work has in recent years been available only to a small number of students.

For the purpose of this chapter, alternatives will be defined as linkages with business beyond the traditional cooperative work experience model—alternative ways to provide students with contacts in the business community that might result in an increased understanding of subject matter or opportunities for career exploration or guidance.

Partnerships between schools and businesses in the private sector have grown rapidly over the past five years and take many shapes and forms. Benefits to schools from partnership activities include (1) increased understanding of the free enterprise system at work; (2) an opportunity for students to explore career options in actual work settings; (3) "hands-on" experiences to prepare students for future employment; (4) an opportunity to enhance the curriculum utilizing business resources, including summer internships for teachers; (5) an opportunity to take advantage of surplus supplies, furniture, or equipment; (6) technical support for the development of computerized programs in such areas as attendance, payroll, or monitoring academic progress of students; (7) financial donations to programs in the form of scholarships or minigrants to teachers; (8) services and products at less expense than if performed in-house or purchased from another supplier; (9) improved student attendance because of involvement with a business volunteer; and finally, (10) building working relationships with the business community. Through partnerships schools gain understanding and respect, and the private sector becomes an ally in support of issues affecting education.

A partnership provides an opportunity for both sides of the collaboration to receive benefit and value from the relationship. That is especially true in school/business partnerships as evidenced by the following examples of how businesses benefit from these activities: (1) Business can stimulate interest in young people in fields where shortages exist, such as science and technology. (2) Through cooperative work programs, employers can field test potential employees and get to know them better prior to providing them full-time employment. (3) Companies spend less on education and retraining when they work closely with the schools to better prepare students for entry-level jobs. (4) Businesses can foster a better understanding of the free enterprise system by developing direct interaction between the schools and businesses. (5) Businesses involved with schools can better understand the specific needs in education and can fill these needs by developing new products and services. (6) Employers have reported that their employees derive personal satisfaction from volunteer work in the schools, resulting in improved morale and improved productivity. (7) Businesses have an opportunity to assist in the development of better citizens. Retail businesses know that if its citizens don't have high ethical standards, expenses are increased as a result of shoplifting, tightened security, etc. (8) Some types of participation provide a tax break for companies. (9) Through involvement in the schools, businesses can develop a greater voice in the community, gain positive recognition for good works, and enhance a reputation as a caring and involved business group.

Partnerships may be developed to fit the individual needs of teachers and students and do not follow a prescribed pattern. However, some common themes emerge that directly relate to business education classrooms.

Career shadowing. Job shadowing, or more importantly, career shadowing, has been increasing rapidly to provide students with an in-depth look at a career of interest on a short-term basis. Usually the student engages in some preliminary investigation of a chosen career prior to engaging in a shadowing experience in order to develop the ability to discuss the career intelligently with a career role model. An ultimate goal for a career shadowing experience is to provide the student an opportunity to verify interest or aptitude for a chosen career. There is no one way to conduct a career shadowing program, but two successful models follow that could be used or modified to meet the individual needs of a classroom teacher.

In one successfully operated program, accounting students are given an opportunity to research a career of interest while the coordinator of the program seeks career role models that are willing to work one-on-one with students in a structured career shadowing program. The identified role model then spends one-half day in the school discussing the career of interest and conducting a mock interview with the student for an entry-level position related to that career. Constructive feedback is given on the student's strengths and weaknesses. This experience is followed by a one-day career shadowing opportunity where the student shadows the role model in his/her job to see what it would be like to work in that chosen occupation. The purpose of this program is to give students an opportunity to verify genuine interest in a chosen career.

Another successful shadowing program taps the resources of a local chamber of commerce to match students with a career role model. Chamber members allow students to shadow them for one-half day in the morning, followed by a special chamber luncheon where students share their experiences and receive a certificate of recognition for participating in the program. The coordinator of this program reports that these experiences have led to summer job opportunities and, in some instances, to financial assistance for attending college or an appropriate form of postsecondary education.

Resource pools. A number of school districts have found it beneficial in a school/business partnership to develop "resource pools" with a variety of business partners. Although business educators have been availing themselves of business resources for years, there is a basic difference in the resource pool concept. An example of a very successful resource pool partnership exists in a suburban school district in St. Louis County. The resource pool staff consists of a coordinator and four facilitators who all work on a part-time basis for the school district. These part-time employees develop the resources in the business community based upon the classroom teachers' needs, schedule the activities, and essentially take care of all the details so that the classroom teacher has nothing left to do except to request the resource. This program began as a pilot program in two elementary schools and was expanded to the current staff who handle more than 700 resources. The resources include a multitude of options—guest speakers, field trips, career-shadowing opportunities, career role models, etc.

Here are some specific business education examples obtained from a resource pool in a "Partners in Education" in Indianapolis, Indiana.

1. Students tour companies with different word processing systems. Some are provided an opportunity to learn a given system and report to the rest of the class. These activities meet a need for students to recognize the variety of word processing systems and to develop transferable skills.

2. Speakers from different retail and wholesale establishments hold a mini-lecture series after which students do a pricing simulation game. These activities meet a need for students to gain a greater understanding of the profit system and how prices are determined.

3. Business representatives work with classes on how to do oral presentations after which students make oral presentations judged by business representatives. These activities meet a need for students to understand the important role communication skills play in the business world.

4. Students divide into groups to visit different kinds of businesses to learn the basics of their accounting systems. Company employees assist students in developing classroom presentations to share with the rest of their accounting class. These activities meet the need for students to recognize different accounting systems and to identify transferable skills learned in their class.

Adopt-A-School. Adopt-A-School programs are popular and may be found in many major cities. An investigation of such programs revealed numerous variations of a central theme underlying adoptions. A good working definition of this form of partnership appeared in a handbook prepared by the Atlanta Public Schools' Adopt-A-School program:

A school/business adoption is a voluntary relationship between one or more business/organizations and a school for the support and enrichment of the educational process. The adoption meets the needs and utilizes the resources of both the school and the business for the benefit of both. Adoptions may be made by any of the following: businesses, governmental agencies, colleges, departments in colleges, hospitals, congregations, social and fraternal organizations, civic and community groups, individuals, consultants, and many others. The following may be adopted: a school, several schools, a grade, department or class in one school or several schools, a program in a school, or a systemwide program. Remember, Adopt-A-School relationships are limited only by the energy and imaginations of the people involved.

Considerable experience has been gained from successful programs in many cities including but not limited to Atlanta, Minneapolis, St. Louis, Dallas, Boston, Kansas City, Baltimore, Cincinnati, Memphis, Chattanooga, and Denver. Smaller communities such as Springfield and Columbia, Missouri, have also been highly successful in developing Adopt-A-School programs. The major differences between an Adopt-A-School relationship and the services provided by a resource pool are the commitment in terms of time and the fact that a variety of resources come from one business partner rather than a variety of sources. An adoption is usually for at least a one-year period, although most adoptions continue on an indefinite basis. Multiple services are provided by the adoptor, and a relationship between the school or department and the adoptor is more personal and long lasting.

One is only limited by imagination when it comes to developing activities that an adopter might provide a business department. For example, consider some of the following activities that might be pursued: organize a career fair; explore and develop interest in nontraditional careers for males and females; organize an employment seminar with speakers on how to develop a resume, how to fill out an application, how to dress for the interview, etc. followed by mock interviews for practice; career-shadowing opportunities; judges for student organization contests; tutors; equipment and training aids; facilities; rewards for student excellence in academic achievement or attendance or whatever needs arise; favors for classroom prizes; field trips; books and magazine donations; training for teachers; an opportunity for students to display their projects in lobbies or cafeterias; "big brother, big sister" relationships where needed; financial assistance for students to travel to leadership conferences; employees to serve on advisory committees, etc. There is no end to the ways in which one might utilize the human resources available from an adoptor.

Specialized school/business partnership options. A number of partnership programs which consist mainly of curriculum materials have been developed and made available either through the national headquarters of a company or through a local distributor. Examples of two programs that might have appeal for business teachers include:

USA Today's CLASSLINE EDUCATION PROGRAM. Curriculum guides are designed with (a) scope and sequence charts to assist teachers in identifying the skills and concepts addressed in specific CLASSLINE lessons; (b) a collection of 'USActivities," 10 in each guide, consisting of a statement of teaching objectives, a step-by-step lesson procedure, and a reproducible student worksheet; (c) a "USActivity Idea Bank" providing additional suggestions for classroom activities for various content areas; and (d) a "USActivity" Teacher's Planning Page and Student Worksheet for writing your own original teaching strategies that you may wish to share with the CLASSLINE Curriculum services. Two specific *USA Today* CLASSLINE programs that are useful for business educators include the "Economics Today" and "USA Careers" units of study. The teaching guides are free, but there is a nominal charge for the newspapers needed by the students. (Order by phone: 1-800-368-3024, x5316.)

MENTOR Law-Related Education Program. This program which originated in New York is now available through the New York Alliance for the Public Schools and the Federal Bar Council (212-510-7507). The developers of the MENTOR program highly recommend training available during the summer for interested teachers partnered with a local lawyer who agrees to assist in developing classroom activities. The basic components of the MENTOR program include an Orientation (lawyers visit the school); Law as a Profession (including related vocations); a Visit to Federal Court (civil litigation emphasis suggested); and a Visit to State Court (criminal law emphasis suggested). Electives (firms and schools are encouraged to add at least one elective to the four basic visits) include Visit to Family Court Judge's chambers, including discussion with social worker; Legal Writing and Research including LEXIS module; or a Lawyer in the Classroom (visit by a local lawyer to school). In addition such activities as a Statewide Mock Trial competition and the Model City Council are available.

SUMMARY

Internships, cooperative programs, and other alternative programs all share one common thread—education beyond the classroom. Such programs have been proven successful. Their visibility in the work force has helped establish much needed networks for future endeavors. Business educators have a rich history of meeting challenges. Continued, innovative efforts will meet the social, educational, and economic needs of a diverse population.

CHAPTER 14

Business Education: A Number One Priority Within the General Curriculum

DONALD L. MOORE

Coronado High School, Colorado Springs, Colorado

RAENELLE HANES

Pikes Peak Community College, Colorado Springs, Colorado

Historically, business education has been receptive to and responded favorably to the demands of its publics. A review of the literature reveals some interesting and enlightening facts to support this statement.

HISTORICAL PERSPECTIVE

The earliest forms of business education were usually through apprenticeship training. In the early Latin grammar schools, where the curriculum was designed for college preparation, business training was sometimes offered in bookkeeping, penmanship, and commercial arithmetic. The inclusion of these offerings in the curriculum came about from the demands of the community. Commercial courses were introduced in 1749 at the Franklin Academy in Philadelphia where the Academy was organized into three divisions, one of which was commercial education. The Academy offered bookkeeping, arithmetic, and other related commercial courses. Some of the other early schools offering courses for commercial careers were the English Classical School for Boys in Boston (1821), Bartlett's Business College in Philadelphia (1832), and Dolber's Commercial School in New York City (1835).

The economic growth that followed the Civil War created a greater demand for commercial curriculums. Business education met this challenge. The invention of the typewriter by Christopher Latham Sholes in 1868 added a new dimension to the commercial curriculum.

During the latter part of the 1880's and the early 1900's, commercial education entered the public schools. Prior to this time, most of the commercial education was in private commercial schools. The offering of commercial education in the public school was a direct result of taxpayer demands that this curriculum be available to students in the public schools.

Although the commercial curriculum was offered, teachers were not yet trained to teach it. Hiring teachers without college training was not readily accepted by the college-trained teachers. Most of the business teachers were products of business/commercial colleges or were hired directly from business. Business education was again meeting the demands of the public.

In 1903 the report of the Committee of Nine (appointed by the National Education Association) recommended that a four-year course of business training be made available in public schools. In 1919 the report of the Federal Board of Vocational Education advocated a plan to provide general clerical training for high school students. Another report of great significance was the Eight-Year Study conducted by a committee of the Commission on Progressive Education Association and College Relations. This 1930 study found that no particular pattern of subjects must be followed in high school in order to assure a student's success in college—traditional curriculums did not prepare students for success in college more adequately than did other curriculums.

Federal legislation assisted commercial education to expand both curriculum and the number of students enrolling. Legislation directly affecting commercial/business education included the Smith-Hughes Act (1917), the George-Deen Act (1937), the George-Barden Act (1946), and the Vocational Act of 1963. The Vocational Act of 1963 was the first time that aid for high school business education was legislated.

Private business colleges experienced the same outstanding growth as the secondary schools during the same period. Demands from business for business graduates added to this growth. The private business colleges became known as independent business schools, and the curriculums were designed to adequately prepare the workers to meet the demands of business in the most efficient manner. As a result, the curriculum was designed to specifically prepare the student for employment.

CURRICULUM

During the 1950's and 1960's, business education curriculums addressed a two-fold purpose—vocational education and general education. Offerings within the curriculum answered the demands of the public: prepare students for entry-level positions in industry, as well as to be wise and informed citizens. The latter focused on the general education of students.

Space exploration turned the nation's interest to more scientific and mathematical training, which negatively affected the business curriculum. However, business education weathered the storm and emerged a viable part of the general curriculum. The "back to the basics" movement and the impact of *A Nation at Risk* also impacted negatively on business education. Flexibility has been the key as business education met the challenges of both these movements to emerge again as an integral part of the general curriculum. During the past 30 to 40 years of reforms and reformers, business educators have been generally complacent, choosing to take a reactive posture, while the curriculum was being greatly affected.

Curriculum insight. The curriculum of the 1990's and beyond must be concerned with the history and historical development of business education. However, with the future of business education hanging in the balance, bold new directions must be taken if business education is to remain a viable and integral component within the comprehensive high school. The Policies Commission for Business and Economic Education believes that business education serves a general as well as a documented occupational need and is one of the most essential programs in the comprehensive high school.

The postsecondary curriculum must also address the issue of business education as general education. The purpose of college/university education is to turn out productive citizens who possess competencies for making worthwhile contributions to society. Business education has always provided these competencies; business education is, and always will be, general education. Efforts must be made to remove the stigma and artificial lines that have separated liberal arts courses from business education courses. A public relations effort must be put in place so that the general public will begin to recognize the true value of business education courses and thereby acknowledge that these competencies exist within business education courses as well as in liberal arts courses.

Educators in both secondary schools and colleges of business are dismayed to hear that businesses are eager to hire liberal arts graduates over business school graduates. If this is true, why would this be? Formal research in the area of employer preferences for liberal arts majors versus business majors is not readily available. However, discussions with employers confirm that they value employees who possess good skills in reading, writing, mathematics, and critical thinking over employees who are weak in these areas.

Postsecondary business educators tell us that many students entering colleges are deficient in the basics. These deficiencies must be dealt with before business content can be mastered. Therefore, not only must technical business courses be taught in colleges, but a foundation of basic academic skills must be laid. College business graduates must go forth ready to compete with the most astute liberal arts graduates. The college curriculum cannot be narrowly focused but must include courses which teach students an appreciation for the past from an historical business perspective, thinking and decision-making skills, ethical behavior, an understanding of our government and how it relates to citizens and business leaders, communication skills, computer skills, a strong foundation in mathematics, psychological principles for good human relations, and technical business skills.

Action versus reaction. Business educators must be proactive, not reactive. Traditionally business educators have passively accepted educational reform realizing that the "new" reform may pass. Many "reforms" in education have done little to truly reform education and have been merely cyclical fads. If true reform is to occur, business educators must assume a more proactive leadership role with regard to the curriculum at all levels.

What actions can be taken and who should be responsible for taking these actions? Business educators have the primary responsibility for being active in the area of curriculum revision and development. They should be taking action at the highest levels of the educational hierarchy, as well as with state and national legislators, to assure that when overall curriculums are reviewed business education is in the forefront.

While there seems to be general agreement on the competencies that an individual must possess to be a productive member of society, considerable disagreement remains over where these competencies are best provided within the curriculum. Business educators must be willing to become more actively involved with time and commitment to show the general public where these competencies are being provided in each of the courses within the business education curriculum.

Business leaders who traditionally hire graduates of the business education curriculum and who have a vested interest in the curriculum must be willing to take a more active role in curriculum revision and development. There must be a greater linkage between business and education than there has been in the past. One method of accomplishing this involvement is through an active advisory committee. Not only should these business leaders be involved as members of vocational advisory committees, they should be involved on committees which advise the designers of the general education curriculum.

Parents and students need to be convinced of the importance of their involvement in the curriculum process. They, too, have a vested interest to ensure that students are not being cheated out of their right to obtain basic business skills as part of their public education.

AN EMERGING CURRICULUM

What will the business education curriculum look like in the future? Will there be courses in the general education curriculum that will encompass content once thought to be specific to business education?

The curriculum of the 1990's and beyond will include more short-term, intensive courses that are in tune with the demands of business and industry. Credit will be given for skills and knowledge acquired through work experience. There will be more cooperation among educational levels. For example, a student who learns to keyboard in junior high school will be accepted into advanced courses such as word processing without having to again "prove" keyboarding ability. Keyboarding and computing skills will be available at all levels from K-12. There will be special courses and programs to effectively meet the needs of the high-risk student.

The use of microcomputers will be integrated into practically every course in the curriculum. The increased use of microcomputers in business will demand proficiency in all aspects of this technology. The microcomputer has replaced the typewriter as the piece of equipment that is the center of instruction in business. Computer applications in every course in the curriculum should be the goal of every program.

The number of courses students will be required to take will undoubtedly increase in the future, and these required courses will include how to use computers, personal finance, the work ethic and the meaning of work, intelligent consumerism, economics and global economics, critical thinking, business ethics, decision making, and oral and written communication. At the heart of this new curriculum will be the intent to make sure that students leave the formal education system with the basics needed to function in a highly technical society. This core of courses may not be labeled as belonging to a particular discipline, and this format may be in the best interest of business education.

Business educators as experts. Business educators will build reputations that will cause them to be thought of as experts in all areas pertaining to business. They may not be the primary deliverers of this instruction at the many levels where these skills will be taught, but they will be the masters who direct and facilitate the delivery of this instruction.

In addition to core courses which contain content traditional to the business education curriculum, a whole new realm of courses must be designed to prepare workers for those jobs in business which are created by new technologies and other changes in the business environment. Many of the courses that have always been in the business education curriculum will still form the nucleus of the curriculum of the future. However, tremendous changes will be made in what is taught in these courses and how they are taught. As more and more content from the traditional business education curriculum is absorbed into the general curriculum, there will be no room for "turfdom." Business educators must think of themselves as educators first and educators for and about business second. As business educators continue to set themselves apart by achieving excellence in their classrooms, the fears of losing courses to other disciplines will no longer be a threat.

Global effect. Business educators and the business education curriculum have perhaps been too narrowly focused. The curriculum of the 1990's and beyond must address global issues. A greater effort must be expended to incorporate a multicultural approach into every course in the curriculum.

INCREASED GRADUATION REQUIREMENTS

Legislative bodies, in response to *A Nation at Risk* and other reported comparative studies of American and foreign students' accomplishments, have attempted to remedy deficiences by legislating that students take more courses in English, science, math, and social studies. Apparently legislators believe that a correlation exists between time spent on a subject and mastery of that subject. A more realistic approach to remedying these deficiencies would be to define desired competencies that must be achieved.

Business education programs have suffered due to increased graduation requirements. Students only have so many hours in the day and cannot schedule business classes because of time restraints brought about by the demands of the increased number of academic classes required by these new graduation requirements.

Answering demands for increased academic skills. Attempts are being made to have business English, business mathematics, and economics fulfill academic graduation requirements. If these courses are to be accepted, business educators must be prepared academically to teach the competencies required to fulfill academic requirements dictated by legislative bodies, accrediting agencies, and colleges/universities.

Scheduling. The expanded school day is one approach that institutions have used to accommodate student requests for business education courses in addition to academic requirements. The number of periods in the day have been increased in order to allow these students the opportunity to take additional or elective classes. While this is an alternative, it has met with some resistance, particularly in those schools where administrators are increasing teacher workloads to accommodate this expanded schedule. In some school districts, teacher workloads have not been increased and students have accepted this concept as an opportunity to participate in elective programs. This is a viable alternative to meeting increased graduation requirements and still having a strong business education program.

Counseling. The role of the counselors and the need for greater interaction between the counselors and business educators becomes paramount in order for students to meet the new graduation requirements and still have room in their schedules for courses which will give them the competencies for functioning in our society which focuses so heavily on business and economics. Business educators must become more effective in communicating to counselors the worthiness of business courses.

Promoting and marketing. Increased academic requirements make marketing and promoting business education more important than ever. New ways must be found to convince students, parents, and the public of the value of courses in the business curriculum. The future of business education depends on an effective marketing program.

EXPANDED DEFINITION OF THE BASICS

Traditionally the basics have been defined as the three R's—"reading, 'riting, and 'rithmetic." However, this definition has changed and will continue to change. The Policies Commission for Business and Economic Education (PCBEE) has expanded the traditional basics to include the "new" basics which are defined as technological skills, decision-making and problem-solving skills, and related employability skills. PCBEE has stated that students with these skills will have the background to cope with new technology.

The new basics were also addressed when randomly selected city supervisors and all 50 state supervisors were asked to comment on the curriculum of the future. The new basics apparently mean different things to different people. This expanded definition of the basics encompasses communication skills, thinking skills, and personal development skills. With these definitions, business educators now have an opportunity to become involved in the change process which includes not only defining the basics but also delineating how business education provides these basics. Business educators must be prepared to take a leadership role in assuring that these new basics are incorporated into the curriculum for the 1990's and beyond.

Business education today has evolved into a discipline which requires teachers to be both generalists and specialists. The current emphasis on the basics demands that business educators assure that students demonstrate competencies in the basic skills if they are to maintain credibility as educators.

No longer can teaching of the three R's be left to other disciplines. If students come into business education programs lacking basic skills, the business educator's responsibility is to teach those skills in addition to the content-specific skills required for success in the job market.

Supervisors' views. Ninety-three state and city supervisors of business education were asked to comment on why business education should be a number one priority within the general curriculum in the 1990's and beyond. A recurrent theme in responses from these people was that business education *is* general education and should, therefore, be used as a vehicle for teaching the basics. Business classes provide opportunities for students to apply basic skills—English, reading, and mathematics. Since these skills are the ones being demanded by the public and by college entrance committees, students should be given credit for attaining them without regard to course title.

Supervisors were in agreement that keyboarding and computer skills should be a priority in the general curriculum. Life skills such as budgeting and job interviewing are all general. English and mathematics skills are taught and reinforced throughout the business curriculum.

Staff reductions due to funding cuts and lower enrollments caused by increased academic requirements for graduation continue to be a problem for business education supervisors. Supervisors agreed that the results of education should be measured by completion of competencies. Simply devoting more hours of instruction in the basics is not necessarily the answer to improvement of basic skills.

Supervisors see a need for statistically documenting the basic academic competencies being developed through the business education curriculum. Better articulation is also a need. Innovation in format and delivery systems is also seen as desirable.

Accountability. Supervisors as well as legislators, educational administrators, and business educators are all concerned about the issue of accountability. Accountability is both a challenge and a threat to business education today. The challenge comes through avenues which demand that business educators be the best that they can be. The threat lies in who determines the factors that will be used to document accountability. Teachers are left trying to please administrators, legislators, parents, students, and the public at large while remaining true to their own values and ideals.

THE CHALLENGE OF CHANGE

Change is inevitable. What can be done to prepare for the changes that must take place in order for business education to lead the way for other disciplines into the exciting future of education. Business educators should be the ones to decide what needs to be changed and then set out to see that the changes are accomplished. Change simply for the sake of change would be a big mistake. Changes should be carefully and selectively thought out. Resistance to change must be dealt with and appropriate groundwork laid well in advance of desired changes. This preparation for change is the key to effectiveness.

Resistance to change is often due to lack of understanding the need for it. Human nature seems to go against making changes recommended by others. Therefore, ownership of ideas for change must be widespread. Ideally, everyone involved in the change process should think that the change was his/her idea. This can be accomplished by involving business and community leaders through advisory committees and encouraging parent groups to participate in developing curriculum and planning for plant and equipment changes.

Business educators must overcome passiveness. A bold stand must be taken where change is needed.

Business education professionals. Tomorrow's business educators will be older because younger people are choosing careers other than education and many young teachers are leaving the profession. At the same time, many students in teacher education programs have left the corporate world at midlife to seek certification and careers in the classroom. These individuals may have a more narrowly focused perspective of student needs, and the general education component of the curriculum may be neglected.

These teachers will be trained in institutions which have a strong emphasis on business and less emphasis on pedagogy. Many teacher education programs are becoming five-year programs with degrees in business and an additional year for courses in methods and student teaching. At the same time, some states have deemphasized the need for methods courses to the extent that individuals are entering the classroom with little or no pedagogical training.

Can teachers without training in pedagogy secure and maintain the interest of students in today's classroom? Teachers today cannot *demand* the respect of students; they must earn it by exhibiting superior intelligence, outstanding knowledge in the content they are teaching, good human relations skills, and the ability to implement psychological principles which result in effective classroom management.

CONCLUSION

Business education will be an important part of the total curriculum of the future. This curriculum will change as society changes, but the basic philosophy of including content to prepare students for jobs in business and providing information about business that will be needed for survival in a business-oriented culture will not change. The business curriculum will no longer be viewed as separate and apart from the academic curriculum; rather, it will be integrated into and accepted as a component of the core of the curriculum at all educational levels.

Promoting and marketing business education will become more important than ever in the 1990's. Students, parents, legislators, and the public at large must be made aware of what is being taught in business programs. Successful graduates may play a significant role in this promotional effort.

College and university demands for increased basic skill levels will cause business educators to place even greater emphasis on basic skills content.

Business educators will be forced to be more aggressive in proving that competencies in the basic skills can be achieved in business classes.

Professional organizations must play a key role in assuring that business education is a number one priority in the 1990's. The leadership of business education professional organizations must be encouraged to pursue a more direct dialogue with other professional organizations so that business education may continue to be foremost in the minds of the professionals in all of these related organizations. Dialogue must also continue with local, state, and national legislators, school boards and state boards of education, and chief executive officers and board members of major corporations.

The 1990's should be an exciting time for business education. With appropriate planning on the part of business educators, business education *will* be a number one priority in the general curriculum.

CHAPTER 15
Trends and Challenges Facing the Goal-Oriented Professional

DOROTHY A. NEAL
Sacopee Valley High School, Cornish, Maine

G.W. MAXWELL
San Jose State University, San Jose, California

Goals get us from one point in our lives to another, serving as guideposts along the well-traveled road of life. Without goals, it is easy to go astray and get nothing accomplished.

Lewis Carroll very appropriately emphasized direction in his famous *Alice's Adventures in Wonderland* when he said:

"Would you tell me, please, which way I ought to go from here?"

"That depends a good deal on where you want to get to," said the Cat.

"I don't much care where—," said Alice.

"Then it doesn't matter which way you go."[1]

Professionals *do* care which way they are going. In order to move forward, professionals must be goal oriented.

Who is today's goal-oriented professional? Today's goal-oriented professional in business education is that person who has a sincere desire and a firm commitment to the profession.

What qualities do goal-oriented professionals possess? Goal-oriented professionals possess a blend of special qualities woven into the fabric of business education. Some of these qualities include: committed, concerned, caring, energetic, enthusiastic, realistic, positive, supportive, and respectful. A professional never loses sight of the goal no matter how far away it may seem to be and attempts to combine the necessary qualities to reach that goal.

Why does the goal-oriented professional succeed? The goal-oriented professional succeeds primarily because of attitude! It has been said many times over that "attitude is the difference between success and failure," and that is truly the case in business education.

Let us approach our specific discussions of the goal-oriented professional in business education keeping in mind these major roles.

---

[1]Carroll, Lewis. *Alice's Adventures in Wonderland.* New York: W.W. Norton and Co., 1971. p. 51.

PROBLEMS OF TODAY'S GOAL-ORIENTED PROFESSIONAL

As we move into the 1990's, we are deluged with information overload. Although we have the technology to make many things happen, without the professional who is willing to change with the times, not much will happen. Technology itself is moving at such a rapid pace that just trying to read current literature can be a totally overwhelming experience.

In addition to reading current literature, there is often a problem *locating* current literature. Because many business teacher education programs have dwindled around the United States, numbers of business educators are dwindling, leaving fewer and fewer professionals to do research.

Futurist articles also are often difficult to locate. Business educators need to focus their attention on the future and should become more involved in reading articles of this type.

Studying and adapting to change has to be one of the greatest challenges for the goal-oriented professional business educator. A large part of being professional is developing an awareness of current trends in the world as well as developing a perspective about what the future may bring.

TRENDS AFFECTING OUR FUTURE

1. Explorations in space are being made primarily by the United States and Russia. Some of the goals are to build a space station, place humans on Mars and possibly even other planets, engage in unmanned exploration of space, and begin business and commercialized use of space.

2. One of the significant attempts to secure food for the world's population is to wrest it from the sea.

3. In biotechnology, experiments concern development of a vast computerized library of human genetic data which can lead to tests, drugs, and treatments for an array of human diseases. The work also involves gene-splicing, a technique enabling insertion of new genes into cells to cure health problems.

4. DNA is being used for investigating individuals' past and for identifying individuals not otherwise identifiable by existing means such as fingerprints. It may even be that human germ cells will be altered to change or remove dangerous genes, for example, those causing cancer.

5. Breakthroughs being sought in medicine include transplanting of almost all human organs and finding a definite cure for AIDS.

6. The world is moving away from communism. China is moving toward a commodity economy wherein goods are made for sale in the marketplace rather than being distributed under a centralized plan. Public ownership continues to be the dominant factor, with market regulation by the state. The Soviet Union is in the midst of altering its system through *perestroika* (restructuring of the economy) and *glasnost* (opening up free discussion).

7. The numbers and proportions of elderly people in the United States continue to increase, bringing on new advances in geriatrics, nursing homes, and retirement homes, as well as developments in the social security and medicare fields.

8. There is much worry and speculation about the long-range future of our globe because of the battering we humans are giving it. The greenhouse effect—in which some of Earth's radiation is trapped, warming the surface, as in a greenhouse—can melt icecaps as the Earth's atmosphere heats up, raise the oceans at the rate of a 1-3 feet a century, and bring on unusually hot summers and unusually severe winters. This in turn can turn continental breadbaskets into arid plains. A major issue is whether or not fossil fuel burning, which puts carbon dioxide into the atmosphere, is widening the hole in the ozone layer. The ozone is Earth's only defense against the effects of potentially harmful ultraviolet radiation from the sun.

A second major question for the future of our world concerns two kinds of population. One kind is ocean pollution. Considerable waste is being dumped into the ocean, such as plastic bottles, plastic bags, and other synthetic materials. Air pollution is a second kind. Pollutants are spewed into the atmosphere from sources such as industrial smokestacks and automobiles. Some pollutants, trapped in water droplets, fall to the earth as acid rain causing such detrimental effects as killing life in lakes, harming forests, corroding buildings, and possibly even jeopardizing our health.

TRENDS AFFECTING THE WORLD OF BUSINESS

1. Robots are increasingly being used to perform production jobs considered too dangerous or monotonous for humans, such as painting, welding, assembling, cleaning up radioactive wastes, bricklaying, installing tunnel linings, and repairing pipeline leaks and blockages. Technological innovations are bringing about amazing improvements in the precision of arm movements and electronic vision systems. The use of robots is even more widespread in Japan than in the United States. We use over half of our robots in the automobile industry.

2. Our economy is experiencing more and more trade on a worldwide basis as evidenced by the burgeoning economies of some Asian nations such as Japan and Korea. Europe is moving to a "United States of Europe," a development geared for completion by 1992. All customs barriers and tariffs will then be eliminated, and Europe will be converted into a single integrated economy with about 325 million customers.

3. Superconductors, when fully employed, can lead to incredible savings in energy. Superconductors cool metals to absolute zero, causing them to lose their electrical resistance. Superconductors could result in magnetic levitation trains speeding at hundreds of miles per hour on a cushion of magnetism, electric cars that are practical and efficient, smaller yet more powerful computers, particle accelerators, and safer reactors operating on nuclear fusion rather than fission.

4. Both our national government's budgetary deficit and its overseas trade deficit have created major uncertainties about the future of our U.S. economy. Solving problems relating to our financial institutions and to the growing numbers of homeless people are other question marks in our future.

5. A trend to watch is "teaching" a computer to "reason" through artificial intelligence, the ability of a computer to combine and manipulate symbols

representing facts and objects in ways that imitate human thought.

6. Future developments in airline transportation will undoubtedly continue. Even now it is possible for supersonic flight to carry us from San Francisco to Toyko or from Chicago to Paris in an hour.

TRENDS DIRECTLY AFFECTING BUSINESS EDUCATION

1. Electronic mail, computer networking, and electronic bulletin boards operate by computers communicating words and/or financial data via phone lines, fiber optics (encasing of a laser beam), microwave, or satellite through hundreds of networks. There are many private member networks, including ADVOCNET, the Adult and Vocational Network in the National Center for Research in Vocational Education at Ohio State University. Others are commercial and may be "rented," such as MCI Communications, AT&T, and GTE Telenet. In either case, they permit tapping myriad bits of information stored in a huge computer or communicating back and forth with other computers.

2. New types of telephones are already in wide use. Many automatically dial programmed numbers, forward calls, record messages, and easily permit conference calls. And on the horizon are wrist-watch telephones and TV telephones.

3. The increasing use of facsimile (fax) machines will compete with use of other traditional delivery systems. Fax machines can speedily impart printed information—words or graphics—from one machine to another in the same building or thousands of miles away.

4. As far as computers are concerned, our challenge is to keep up with the latest developments, such as optical storage disks, reduced-instruction-set computers (RISC) needing fewer instructions from memory than do conventional computers, parallel processing (much faster than serial processing), and scientific supercomputers.

5. The role of women in our working society continues to increase. According to the Bureau of Labor Statistics, almost half of all U.S workers are women and over half of all mothers and wives in the United States are working. Of all persons employed in managerial and professional specialty positions, almost half are women. A major negative aspect is that women's wage rates are presently only about two-thirds of men's. Child care for working mothers is a rapidly growing and changing concern. The future will undoubtedly see new directions in child care facilities.

6. Training within industry is a trend that has been with us for years but continues to increase and grow in importance. School education is being increasingly supplemented by industry-taught courses which range from the basics to advanced technology.

WHAT LIES AHEAD IN THE MORE DISTANT FUTURE?

Who, for example, can answer these and other questions about what might happen 50-100 years from now; Will warring nations destroy themselves (possibly even the world) by nuclear war? Will explorations in space result in placement of colonies of humans in space? What will be the source or combination of sources of our power; nuclear energy, solar energy, fossil fuel energy, flowing water, and/or hot subsurface rocks? Will robots some day really help us do housework? What will be the medicines of the future? Will medicines be developed that give us more energy, extend our lives, and improve our intelligence and our memory? How much longer will be life expectancy? Will third-world nations ever emerge in the future from their present poverty situations? Will some jobs that used to be the "backbone" of business education, such as file clerk and secretary, disappear? What new jobs (as a result of technology) will be created in their place? Will we work fewer hours than we do now? Will we work more in our homes?

SUGGESTIONS FOR GOAL-ORIENTED PROFESSIONALS IN A WORLD OF CHANGE

Professional organizations provide business educators with the opportunity to read literature, apply learning to classroom instruction, develop curriculum, and meet other colleagues through conferences. When a business educator becomes involved in a professional association as an active member, new opportunities often present themselves. For example, a business educator may work on a committee, become an officer, assist in projects that will benefit the profession, or even write an article for an association's professional journal or other publication.

Another avenue of professional involvement for business educators is working directly in the business world. Business educators should obtain actual work experience in the business world prior to teaching and continue to do so throughout their professional life. This is one of the best ways to keep abreast of changing trends. An example of this is the partnership NBEA formed with Manpower Inc. to provide business educators with this opportunity to work directly in the business world during the summers.

Business educators should also take an active role in government at the local, state, regional, and national levels. By writing letters to elected representatives a business educator is letting them know personal feelings concerning matters that directly affect business education. Business educators should also work in person to directly influence elected representatives who can assist them in projects affecting business education.

Business educators must constantly be on the alert for change and current trends which lead to future developments. Several avenues provide opportunities for doing so:

- *Conferences.* Business education associations can include and even highlight futurists on conference programs.
- *Research.* Those pursuing advanced degrees can undertake master's and doctoral studies that deal with pertinent future trends and attempt to analyze their effect on business education. Studies in futurism might also be commissioned by Delta Pi Epsilon.

- *Publications.* Professional business education periodicals and yearbooks can include special series of articles or even special issues dealing with futurism.

PROFESSIONAL INVOLVEMENT BY BUSINESS EDUCATION ASSOCIATIONS

Business education associations should be professionally involved in matters that affect the present and future welfare of the field.

1. In addition to their regular programs, business education associations should continue to organize special conferences built around and dealing solely with single and specific topics (e.g., current and future needs of business education). Some conferences of this type have been restricted, with invitations extended only to selected persons. Others have been open to any and all interested business educators, business representatives, and publishers.

2. There should be even further "cross-referencing" of business education associations and professional associations related to business education. A few examples of these associations are:

Administrative Management Society, 2360 Maryland Road, Willow Grove, PA 19090

Association of Records Managers and Administrators, 4200 Somerset, Suite 215, Prairie Village, KS 66208

The Association of Business Communication, England Building, University of Illinois, 608 South Wright Street, Urbana, IL 61801

Data Processing Management Association, 606 Busse Highway, Park Ridge, IL 60068

Professional Secretaries International, 301 East Armour Boulevard, Kansas City, MO 64111

The World Future Society, 4916 St. Elmo Avenue, Bethesda, MD 20814

Professional activities could include developing joint projects by two or more associations, holding joint association meetings or conferences, and having representatives of one association serve as representatives or even officers of another association.

3. Business education associations should continue to strive to develop close relationships with business and industry. Asking prominent business executives to serve on the executive boards of business education associations is one possibility, although sometimes difficult to achieve. Working with business firms on matters of common interest, such as curriculum and internships, is another suggestion.

CLOSING STATEMENT

Today's goal-oriented professional in business education must continue to develop professionalism in all activities undertaken. The future belongs to the professional who has the power to envision a goal and uses the vision to achieve the goal.

CHAPTER 16

Business Education in the 1990's—
A Window of Opportunity

WILLARD R. DAGGETT
ROBERT A. JAFFARIAN
New York State Education Department, Albany

The 1980's have been challenging years for business education throughout the United States. Like other areas of vocational education, business education has spent the decade trying to respond to fundamental changes in the economy and in society in general. Technological innovation, changing demographics, new underpinnings for the economy, and changing aspirations of female students are all contributing to a transformation of society. At the same time, business education in many schools has been coping with new graduation requirements and the introduction of new curriculums to keep pace with the changing world of work. How well business education can continue to adapt to ongoing change will determine the role it will play in preparing students for their adult lives. If the role is to be a leading one, then business educators must have a clearly articulated vision of the future to guide them.

CHANGES AND CHALLENGES OF THE 1980'S

Technology has been causing fundamental structural changes in all sectors of the economy. The kinds of jobs that are available and the way the work is organized and performed has been profoundly influenced by technology. Today companies all over the country are spending substantial amounts of money to upgrade the skills of office workers so that they can perform new tasks made possible by technology.

The U.S. economy is now primarily based on information and services. In this economy, people have become the driving force behind economic growth. Building human capital has to be a national priority as the population ages. There are fewer young people to move into the labor market, and a greater number of them lack the educational background for success in today's job market. Competition is growing among industries for the same pool of workers. Office work is not attracting a sufficient number of new employees and those hired often lack adequate skills. Polls indicate that the top two goals of students of both sexes as the 1980's draw to a close are challenging careers and substantial personal income, quite a change from polls of the 1970's in which females rate marriage and family as their highest priorities. Many new employment opportunities have become available to women.

Neither students nor their parents consider office employment, as it has traditionally been structured, a viable career option for attaining financial rewards and getting ahead.

Conditions within the educational community itself during the decade have posed additional challenges to business education. The educational reform movement that swept the country in the mid 1980's increased graduation requirements in many schools. As a result, the amount of class time teachers have with students has decreased along with opportunities for students to take subjects such as business education as electives. Coupled with the general decline in the secondary population, new school requirements and competition with other disciplines which have also introduced computers have had an adverse effect on enrollment in business education programs.

The 1980's have not been easy years for business educators, especially those who have also witnessed significant change in the courses they teach. The schools which have instituted new, computer-based curriculums in business education in response to changing office practices will find themselves well positioned to meet the new challenges of the 1990's if they have focused on teaching basic concepts and principles of computers and information systems. Like all other business educators, however, they too will have to rethink the mission of business education in preparing students for a dramatically different world of work.

LOOKING AHEAD TO THE 1990'S

The decade of the 1990's will bring continued and accelerated structural changes in the U.S. economy, labor force, and way of life, spurred on by new technologies. Technological change is occurring faster and faster. In the 1950's, a change from one type of equipment or technology to another took 10 to 12 years. It has been predicted that in 1992-95, technological changes will take place every three to six months.

Throughout these waves of change, business will remain the absolute growth field in terms of employment because of the enormous increase in information-related occupations. Even today information-related jobs are no longer only in office settings but on the floor of the manufacturing plant, in the laboratories and at the bedside in the health care industry, and in the kitchens of fast food establishments. The U.S. Department of Labor predicts that by the year 2000, 44 percent of jobs will be in collecting, analyzing, synthesizing, storing, or retrieving data.

American offices are in the process of a transformation which will have a substantial impact on where office work will be performed, who will perform it, and how it will be performed in the 1990's. The office has moved away from its traditional role as a support service to become a primary business department. Offices serve as the nerve centers for business and other organizations which have become heavily dependent on information systems. Word processing, data processing, reprographics, and communications will be integrated into a function made up of many interdependent, complementary units and networks that permit speedier information gathering and flow as

well as improved management capabilities. Through networking, the office can function as the primary center of a business, linking systems and workstations together.

As the functions of the office are transformed, so too are the roles and responsibilities of the workers in the office. Computers have changed both the nature of work and the worker. Support roles, the traditional focus of business education, are becoming primary roles in the business workplace. Secretaries and support staff are using computers and networking to do many tasks formerly delegated to specialists. Skill in operating information systems is also important for professionals, managers, and supervisors. Yet, increasingly, the most sophisticated work is being done by support staff upon whom the professions must rely to show them how to use the database and information system. In a reversal of roles, the professional or manager is beginning to operate the keyboard to enter first generation documents and data; the support staff member or secretary then updates and refines the data. The person able to manipulate elements of a network system will continue to play a primary role in the operation of a business.

Knowledge of information systems has become a basic skill necessary for all future business occupations at every level. Support staff must be able to retrieve and manipulate all kinds of information in a complex system (e.g., electronic mail, electronic filing, database management). Support staff members will also need an enormous increase in their general knowledge of the business in which they work. In the office of the 1990's, there will be a critical need for greater flexibility in terms of job classification, promotions, and tasks that individuals may perform.

The capability of information systems and technology to perform an ever expanding and far-reaching series of tasks will be critical to the future of the United States. Labor is no longer an economic commodity. The cost of labor in this country is too high in comparison with other countries. By using satellite transmission, U.S. companies can employ less expensive labor for computer applications of manual tasks. So how can American business remain competitive globally in the information processing field? The answer lies in using more sophisticated information systems to process virtually all work. Technology-based employment has become the United States' economic commodity. Business education cannot continue to prepare students for relatively dead-end, labor-intensive tasks that may quickly become obsolete or can be accomplished more cheaply elsewhere. The opportunity and capability exist to ready students for primary roles within business.

Historically, office work has been in the low-wage sector of the economy and opportunities for advancement in an organization have been extremely limited. The outlook is beginning to change, however. Worker shortages are causing salaries to rise in a variety of industries, and the office equipment field will have to follow suit to remain competitive. Furthermore, the new tasks and responsibilities of office workers in the 1990's will require employees with higher level skills. To attract capable employees, business/industry and, to a smaller extent, state government are beginning to build clear career

advancement paths that enable competent workers to progress to new job titles and higher salary levels.

A VISION OF THE FUTURE FOR BUSINESS EDUCATION

Business education is at a crossroads as the 1990's approach. The changes in society, the economy, and business practices that began in the 1980's are paving the way for a decade very different from the past. Business education needs to continue its role in preparing students for their personal lives, postsecondary education, and for employment. Its role in the latter, preparing students for employment, needs to be reevaluated. Business education must rethink its mission by asking first what kinds of jobs it is preparing students for and then how business education can deliver the necessary preparation. The responses to these questions form the basis for creating a vision of business education in the 1990's.

Business education used to be designed around the manual tasks by which information was processed in the office setting. These manual tasks have been replaced by faster and more efficient computer applications, and thus, business education moved to teaching these computer applications. Now the business community is moving beyond simple applications to the use of computers for all information needs. Complex systems are in use that are much more than the computerization of manual tasks. Business education will thrive only by designing its programs around the complex information processing systems that are fast dominating the business world.

Business education in the 1990's must be perceived and operated as a program that provides information for and about business, including such areas as the private enterprise system, financial services provided by business, legal aspects of business, risk-sharing, and management. Business education should provide students with an understanding of the organization and operation of American business activities in the context of the global marketplace. Viewed in this way, business education is a broad and diverse discipline that should be part of the general education of all students as well as offering job specific skills for the workplace.

Modernizing existing business education programs to make them more responsive to the changing attitudes and aspirations of students and to accommodate the changing nature of the labor market and the influx of technology is not enough. A plan for simply updating current programs fails to account for the profound changes taking place in where, when, and how people work. These fundamental structural changes in the world of work must be met by fundamental structural changes in business education.

Business education must take a total systems approach rather than a task-oriented approach to information processing. The ongoing evolution of information handling will increase reliance on interactive and multi-functional hardware, software, and integrated office systems. As the growing use and sophistication of information systems transforms support roles into primary roles, so too must business education begin to prepare its students for these primary roles.

Tomorrow's work environment will involve jobs that are always in transition, with changing equipment, work tasks, and responsibilities. Students who enter the work force upon graduation from high school must be prepared for periodic changes in jobs and work assignments. Business education will not be able to train its students on the latest equipment; technology is evolving too fast for that. Business education must focus on teaching the skills, concepts, and systems which underlie all pieces of technology. The educational preparation must also emphasize critical and analytical thinking skills, responsibility, flexibility, and the work ethic. Students who are thoroughly trained in these basics will be capable of adapting to new equipment and should be able to find meaningful work in business or in other fields.

A NEW AGENDA FOR BUSINESS EDUCATION

Change will be the password to success for business education programs in the 1990's. First, business education has to change its historical mind-set— that its mission is to prepare students for support roles in business and industry. These support roles may cease to exist in the next decade, replaced by primary roles requiring the use of sophisticated technology for analyzing and manipulating data and an understanding of business organization and operations. Second, business educators must change the public perception of business education as a discipline that prepares students for repetitive, low-wage jobs.

With a technology-based curriculum responsive to workplace requirements, business education can broaden its constituency to include a greater proportion of high school students. All students need a multifaceted program to meet the demands of an information/technology age. Shifts will continue to occur in the U.S. labor market in terms of jobs available and skills required, but a few skills will be relevant to the entire employment sector—keyboarding, data manipulation, problem solving/decision making, understanding information systems and other technological systems, resource management, the economics of work, applied math and science, career planning. Business education must seize these skills and teach them to students.

New curriculums must concentrate on the development of strong skills in business communications, keyboarding, information processing, data analysis, data manipulation, and understanding of integrated office systems, while deemphasizing shorthand, machine transcription, comprehensive data processing, and office procedures courses. Academic credit should be given for communications skills integrated in the curriculum and for desktop publishing and graphics content in fulfillment of art requirements.

Business courses need to reflect the actual conduct of business in the United States. Given the increasing dependency of business on more efficient and effective information management systems, students need to understand systems and their role in business organizations. They must be able to identify relationships among system components and trace information and work flow. In addition, students need to understand theoretical concepts of business

organization and management. A program combining basic skills applicable to all occupational levels plus an innovative systems approach responsive to workplace changes will equip business education students to assume primary roles in the work setting.

An important item on the new agenda for business education will be the revitalization of teacher education. In this effort, teacher educators will have to take the leading role. They can begin by reforming and updating teacher education curriculums so that they focus on the office as a primary rather than support operation and emphasize such areas as information systems and broad, transferable skills. A few universities have already begun the process of reorienting their business teacher education programs. NBEA's Task Force on Business Teacher Education Model Curriculum has developed a curriculum guide that can be used for this purpose.

Communicating the new mission of business education to the largest possible audience will be vitally important. Business teachers must take the lead by becoming very active spokespersons for the new program. Business, community groups, boards of education, guidance counselors, parents, and students must be informed of the changes in business education. Successful and enthusiastic students also make excellent spokespersons. Through creative approaches and activities, business teachers must see that the message about the new direction of business education is heard and understood by all target groups.

A TIME FOR LEADERSHIP

The future of business education rests in the hands of business teachers, administrators, and teacher educators. During the 1990's, business educators will either manage the decline of their discipline or oversee a fundamental structural change in the discipline. If changes are not made in response to new economic conditions and workplace requirements, business education will witness an exodus of students from its programs.

A dramatic increase both in the importance of business education in the school curriculum and in enrollments in programs can occur if appropriate changes are made. In business, the office has changed from a support role to a primary role. Likewise, business education can move from a support role in the educational system to a primary role if it has the courage to abandon some of its past practices.

Business education should continue to be the prime deliverer of instruction dealing with information systems. It must be understood, however, that these information systems are no longer based on labor-intensive tasks but rather on the basic concepts, principles, and systems of technology. Integrated information systems must become the focus of business education programs.

Can business education change? It will not be easy, but the economic and human consequences for students and for U.S. businesses in their ability to be competitive in the global economy will be disastrous if changes are not made. Everyone involved in business education in the 1990's must be prepared to lead, to follow, or to get out of the way.